FEAR

HENRY W. WRIGHT

Be in Health GLOBAL
4178 Crest Highway
Thomaston, Georgia 30286

www.beinhealth.com

EAN: 978-1-934680-34-6

Disclaimer

This ministry does not seek to be in conflict with any medical or psychiatric practices nor do we seek to be in conflict with any church and its religious doctrines, beliefs or practices. We are not a part of medicine or psychology, yet we work to make them more effective, rather than working against them. We believe many human problems are fundamentally spiritual with associated physiological and psychological manifestations. This information is intended for your general knowledge only. Information is presented only to give insight into disease, its problems and its possible solutions in the area of disease eradication and/or prevention. It is not a substitute for medical advice or treatment for specific medical conditions or disorders. You should seek prompt medical care for any specific health issues. Treatment modalities around your specific health issues are between you and your physician.

As pastors, ministers and individuals of this ministry, we are not responsible for a person's disease, nor are we responsible for his or her healing. All we can do is share what we see about a problem. We are not professionals; we are not healers. We are only ministers administering the Scriptures, and what they say about this subject, along with what the medical and scientific communities have also observed in line with this insight. There is no guarantee that any person will be healed or any disease be prevented. The fruit of this teaching will come forth out of the relationship between the person and God based on these insights, given and applied. This ministry is patterned after the following scriptures: 2 Corinthians 5:18-20; 1 Corinthians 12; Ephesians 4; Mark 16:15-20.

Preface

This booklet was developed from a teaching to a live audience and has been kept in a conversational format. It is designed to reach a personal level with the reader rather than present a structured, theological presentation. Many times the reader will feel that Henry Wright is talking directly to him or her. The frequent use of the pronoun *you* is meant to penetrate the human heart for conviction, not for accusation. Pastor Henry has been called to the office of pastor, and as such, he takes care of God's flock (whereas one called to the office of teacher does not take care of the sheep).

CONTENTS

**FOR GOD HATH NOT GIVEN US
THE SPIRIT OF FEAR; BUT OF POWER,
AND OF LOVE, AND OF A SOUND MIND.**

2 TIMOTHY 1:7

FEAR

Introduction

God gave us emotions to enhance our lives. The emotion fear was intended to alert us to danger so that we may respond by our fight or flight abilities.

However, much of mankind lives with Fear* on a daily basis. *Every one of us has been subjected to Fear.* It may have been Fear of tomorrow, Fear of Failure, Fear of the unknown or Fear of spiders. Perhaps it was Fear working in us as anxiety. Perhaps we think of it as stress, the modern term for what the Bible refers to as Fear.

Many lives are ruled by Fear. This kind of Fear was not given to us by God. This kind of Fear does not warn us or protect us. This kind of Fear brings destruction

This Fear is a spirit. It is an evil spirit. Fear is an antichrist spirit. It is an unclean, Unloving* spirit because it tells you that you are not accepted and not loved by God. But the Word says you *are* loved. Any thought that comes to

---

* Fear and other strong men are capitalized because they are names of entities in the kingdom of darkness.

you from another voice or from your own thought process *which contradicts the Word of God* is an antichrist thought. Jesus is the Word and anything that disagrees with Him is anti-Jesus or antichrist; *every thought.*

That is why 2 Corinthians says,

> **Casting down imaginations, and every high thing that exalteth itself against the knowledge of God, and bringing into captivity every thought to the obedience of Christ;**
>
> 2 Corinthians 10:5

This ministry began in the early 80s when it seemed God was not answering prayer. God began to reveal that there could be spiritual roots and blocks.

God is not going to answer your prayer if you will not get these problems straightened out in your life. He won't answer "when fear cometh, when distress and anguish" are tormenting you because "you hated knowledge, and did not choose the fear of the Lord: You would have none of His counsel; you despised all His reproof. Therefore shall you eat of the fruit of your own way, and be filled with your own devices." Proverbs 1:25, 29-31

God has told you not to fear. If you allow Fear to rule your life, then you may have a disease that will come because of your inability to believe and trust God. When your desolation comes, do you think God is going to answer your prayer to heal you, but let you keep the Fear that is causing your problem? He is not, because He would have to be unholy to do that.

In other words, He would have to bless you and let you keep your sin. Your disease would come back anyway, because the wages of that sin are still death and are still the problem. God is dealing with this situation in the following scripture.

20Wisdom crieth without; she uttereth her voice in the streets:

21She crieth in the chief place of concourse, in the openings of the gates: in the city she uttereth her words, ***saying,***

22How long, ye simple ones, will ye love simplicity? and the scorners delight in their scorning, and fools hate knowledge?

23Turn you at my reproof: behold, I will pour out my spirit unto you, I will make known my words unto you.

24Because I have called, and ye refused; I have stretched out my hand, and no man regarded;

25But ye have set at nought all my counsel, and would none of my reproof: Proverbs 1:20-25

Wisdom is crying in the streets in verse 20. God has given us His Word to bring us to a place of safety. If God has told you to forgive your neighbor but you will not, don't be too upset when the diseases coming out of Bitterness hit your life. When you hang onto Unforgiveness, there is a disease that will come.

What if the result of Fear is malabsorption? What if mitral valve prolapse is a result of Anxiety? What are you going to do with that?

What about fibromyalgia? What are you going to have to lay down first? The fibromyalgia or the Fear? You cannot lay down the fibromyalgia until you get right with God in the area of Fear. Do you see what He is saying here?

When we help you recognize roots of disease and blocks to healing in whatever disease you are dealing with, we are paving the way for you to be free. Then you can call unto God according to knowledge, not according to ignorance. We bring you knowledge and wisdom so you can recover yourself from the snare of the devil. We gain knowledge of God from the Word of God.

> **So then faith *cometh* by hearing, and hearing by the word of God.**
> Romans 10:17

You either believe the Word, or you do not believe the Word. If you do not believe it, you have a spirit of Unbelief. If you *cannot* believe it, you may have an antichrist spirit which is either mind control, Witchcraft, or some other occultic spirit guide that has been assigned to you. You may have been programmed in your thinking by doctrines of devils through false teaching.

You are fertile ground. You are a sponge in the spiritual dimension and in the thinking dimension. You are just like a multi-band receiver radio. You are receiving different voices at all levels and all dimensions. The Bible says there are many voices.

> **There are, it may be, so many kinds of voices in the world, and none of them *is* without signification.**
> 1 Corinthians 14:10

They all have something significant to say, but what they are saying does not always match what God has said.

Paul in 2 Corinthians 10:5 told us to hold thoughts in captivity if they do not match what God has said. When you catch that thought, grab hold of it and do not let it go any further. Has Fear made a mess of your life? Have Fear and anxiety tried to destroy your family tree? They also want to destroy your posterity.

A DEMAND TO BE FULFILLED

Hebrews 11:6 says, "Without faith, it is impossible to please God," because faith represents your future. Fear represents the *destruction* of your future.

Faith and Fear are equal in this dimension: both demand fulfillment. Faith will always defeat Fear, because faith is a work of the Holy Spirit. Fear is a work of the created being named Lucifer, who fell and became Satan. He now rules a kingdom determined to destroy mankind.

This kingdom consists of many principalities and powers, rulers of the darkness of this world and spiritual wickedness in high places. They dwell in the 2nd heaven.

Fear is from that kingdom. Fear is Satan's attempt to overthrow God's plan in the earth, using you to do it. Feelings cannot be trusted.

Your hopes motivate you because that is what faith is. Faith involves God's plan for you: what He created for you from the foundation of the world.

Some churches preach what is called a faith message. But no one can live up to the faith message, because it is really a system of works. It is a form of Witchcraft, due to the manipulation and control motivations. They use the Word of God to manipulate and control their circumstances.

There is nothing wrong with using the Word. The Word of God is true and faith is true, but the faith teaching is based on works. They teach your well-being is based on how much faith you have and how you are using the Word to get what you want. Faith is not works.

> **Now faith is the substance of things hoped for, the evidence of things not seen.** Hebrews 11:1

Faith is that simple. Your hopes need to be based on the known will and knowledge of God for mankind in the earth, as revealed by the Word of God. Knowing the will of God requires reading His Word, because it tells you what

His plans are for mankind. An example of God's will is, "If at all possible, live peaceably one with another."

> **If it be possible, as much as lieth in you, live peaceably with all men.** Romans 12:18

Another scripture tells us to stay away from those who equate gain with godliness.

> **Perverse disputings of men of corrupt minds, and destitute of the truth, supposing that gain is godliness: from such withdraw thyself.** 1 Timothy 6:5

There is a large movement that teaches the more you have, the more blessed you are, and the more spiritual you are, the closer to God you are. That is the 'name it and claim it' group, the 'seed faith giving' group. "You pay me and I will move God's hand for you."

That is the same as the sale of indulgences that has been around for hundreds of years. "You pay me five dollars: I will get God to do something for you." "You give me a hundred: God will give you a thousand." That is the manipulation of Witchcraft and Occultism.

The Bible says,

> **But seek ye first the kingdom of God, and his righteousness; and all these things shall be added unto you.** Matthew 6:33

Some people struggle with what they hear on TV because it is a mish mash. One teacher says this and another contradicts it. No wonder the church is confused. I find if I read the Word and obey it, I stay on target with what God has called me to do. It is important to prove everything from the Word. [And that includes this teaching.]

Timothy says we are to turn away from those who say gain is godliness, but then he goes on to say,

But godliness with contentment is great gain. 1 Timothy 6:6

Many people chasing health and wealth are tormented by drivenness. These are people trying to create their own blessings. Fear is motivating them, not faith.

Fear will try to create your future. It projects into the future, based on your past. It is important that you learn to put aside everything you have been exposed to that controls you and tries to create your future for you. That could include recognizing what is in your family tree, your memes, philosophies, idiosyncrasies and any programming for victimization.

"Faith is the substance of things hoped for, the evidence not yet seen." This statement, "the evidence not yet seen," represents the future. Faith is *substance*. When you touch your fingers, you know they are there. You can feel them. They are *substance* and they are real. **Faith** is the *substance* of things hoped for that has not happened yet. Fear is the same as faith in that dimension. It has substance. **Fear** is the substance of things *not* hoped for, the evidence *not* yet seen.

Faith and Fear are Equal

What you are meditating on or thinking about every day occupies your mind. You may be meditating on the good things or you may be thinking about all the things that will go wrong in your life today and tomorrow. The object of your fear is not only being projected into tomorrow, but also yesterday's projected fear is here today. Then your days become nights and your nights become days.

The Bible says,

> **...God hath dealt to every man the measure of faith.**
>
> Romans 12:3

When I was a kid learning to ride a bicycle without training wheels, I toppled a few times. When I went down, I had a decision to make, because my knee was hurting. Either I would let the experience of falling down and banging up my knee become fear that would make me quit, or I would pass through that and become experienced so that I would not fall down. I made a choice. I climbed back on my bicycle because that was my faith. My hope to conquer riding my bike was stronger than my fear.

Faith defeats Fear

Some people go from fear to faith faster than others. Some people are accelerated and walk away from these issues of fear in no time. Others are like the old plodding mule train. It is a caravan and they are going to get there one day. The first line is already down to the oasis and has been sitting there sipping iced tea for hours when you come plodding on in with your mule train. Everyone is different and you must not judge yourself by another. Judge yourself only by who you are in creation and by the Word of God. Everyone's family problems are different.

There is no guarantee what you are believing for will ever happen, nor is there a guarantee what you fear will ever happen. Sometimes we give more power to our fear than to our faith. The Bible has a lot to say about tomorrow.

Take therefore no thought for the morrow: for the morrow shall take thought for the things of itself. Sufficient unto the day *is* the evil thereof. Matthew 6:34

And he said unto his disciples, Therefore I say unto you, Take no thought for your life, what ye shall eat; neither for the body, what ye shall put on. Luke 12:22

Be careful for nothing; but in every thing by prayer and supplication with thanksgiving let your requests be made known unto God. Philippians 4:6

Casting all your care upon him; for he careth for you. 1 Peter 5:7

These scriptures teach us how to deal with worry and anxiety. There is not one person who does not have to face fear issues, because Fear is a ruling power. Satan's kingdom is knocking at your door all the days of your life on this planet. But it does not have to control you and it does not have to rule you.

When Jesus was tempted in the wilderness the devil was defeated by the Word. Then he left Jesus for a season. The evil one tried to tempt Jesus, but he found nothing in Jesus that would yield to evil.

Hereafter I will not talk much with you: for the prince of this world cometh, and hath nothing in me. John 14:30

When Fear comes knocking at your door, make sure you do not have the corresponding spirit of anxiety to link with it. Bitterness must be gone, Envy and Jealousy must be gone, Rejection must be gone and the unclean, Unloving spirit must be gone.

Matthew says,

> **Therefore I say unto you, Take no thought for your life, what ye shall eat, or what ye shall drink; nor yet for your body, what ye shall put on. Is not the life more than meat, and the body than raiment?** Matthew 6:25

Some of the common fruits of the spirit of Fear are panic attacks and phobias.

Luke 13:4 tells us there was a high-rise building that collapsed and 18 men died. Jesus was asked the question, "Lord, were the 18 men that died in this tragedy more evil than the rest of the people in the town and therefore God's judgment fell on them?"

Jesus said, "The issue is not whether they were more evil than the rest of the people. The issue is this: *Are you right with God*?" If you are right with God, then you have no Fear of Death and dying because Paul said, "To be absent from the body is to be present with the Lord." 2 Corinthians 5:8

There are examples in the Word where God took people at an early age. It is not often, but God is sovereign. There was a young man in the Old Testament whose father was a very evil king. God looked down from heaven, saw the heart of this young man and wanted that young man forever. The family was very evil. The Bible says God took him, because if the young man had been allowed to live, he would have been perverted and the goodness of his heart would have become evil. Then God would have lost him forever.

The relationship God had with Elijah was such that he did not die. God just took him.

TWO DIMENSIONS OF FEAR

The Spirit of Fear is a principality. A principality is like a head architect who is in charge, with additional Fear beings underneath that have specific assignments.

There are two dimensions of Fear. One is that Fear is an evil spirit. It can become difficult to separate yourself from that spirit, so you become one in spirit and soul with the spirit of Fear.

The other dimension is that the fruit of Fear becomes part of you biologically. *It is possible to become programmed in your mind to have a personality of fear and it has nothing to do with an evil spirit.* Both dimensions must be resolved. The mind must be renewed and purged of the old beliefs that represent Fear.

When you have been around Fear for so long that you have become phobic and panic-ridden, mere exposure to your Fear stressor puts your body into a Fear reality. An evil spirit of Fear doesn't have to be present because the preprogramming rules your response. That is the mind-body connection.

The book of Hebrews says,

> **For the word of God *is* quick, and powerful, and sharper than any twoedged sword, piercing even to the dividing asunder of soul and spirit, and of the joints and marrow, and *is* a discerner of the thoughts and intents of the heart.**
>
> Hebrews 4:12

The antidote to the principality of Fear is very simple. Trust God. Fear is an antichrist spirit because it says you cannot trust God. It says evil is more powerful than God.

Job 13:15 says, "Even though God slay me, yet will I trust Him." God did not slay Job. It was not His intention to do so. Job could say that because he came to a place of trust. Job decided to trust God, yet in that great confrontation when he was extolling his own righteousness and values, God just appeared in the room and said, "Where were you, big boy?"

Job had a little spiritual pride. He was chief in the ways of God. He was an upright man. But in Job we see Leviathan is the king over the children of pride and Behemoth is chief in the ways of God.

> **Canst thou draw out leviathan with an hook...** Job 41:1

> **He beholdeth all high *things*: he *is* a king over all the children of pride.** Job 41:34

> **Behold now behemoth, which I made with thee...** Job 40:15

> **He *is* the chief of the ways of God: he that made him can make his sword to approach *unto him*.** Job 40:19

Leviathan and Behemoth are two principalities that fueled what Job feared the most. And what Job feared the most came upon him. He lost his children because they were party animals. Job was afraid they might sin in some way and upset God, so he was going around mopping up the spiritual dust. He did not believe God could sustain them.

Let me encourage you to *release your children to God* once and for all. Pray for them. Do not be in fear concerning them. Just pray for them.

Release your children to God

Knowing God and knowing His Word will not guarantee your freedom. The church is full of people who can quote scripture forwards and backwards, but the Scriptures are not bearing fruit in their lives. We have been taught to be intellectually and spiritually superior, but we have not been taught how to defeat our enemy.

The Word is Jesus Christ, a living being, but the defeat of your enemy with the Word can only be fruitful if you *believe* and *make it part of your life*. It is not fruitful if you believe God because of works, because of mythologies, or because of science. You have to become *one* with God: His nature and your nature have to become one in that area of your life. To become one with the Word is to know what the living being, Jesus Christ, has said as revealed in the Scriptures and believe it.

When His thoughts become your thoughts, you are spiritually changed. When His ways become your ways, you are spiritually changed.

Job's biggest spiritual problems were in three areas and they were an open door for Satan to come and oppress him. One was fear, the second was personal pride and the third was spiritual pride. There is a difference between personal pride and spiritual pride.

Spiritual pride is the spirit of religion, the Pharisaical way of thinking. It is Luciferian in thought. Personal pride is where you think there is nothing spiritually wrong with you and you are in denial.

The Fear-Faith Counterfeit

Faith is according to knowledge, not according to fear-faith. Where there is faith, there is also a counterfeit. Fear-faith is a dangerous spirit because it counterfeits real faith. You are not asking God out of simple belief; you are asking God out of a fear-need. You will not receive anything from God out of fear-need. Philippians 4:6 says to let your supplications be made known unto God. It does not say to let them be known in fear.

Fear-faith is a counterfeit of real faith. Fear-faith approaches God out of fear and out of need, not out of faith, not out of real believing. Fear-faith will make you quote 14 scriptures a day *hoping* it will work. Fear-faith will get you running to ministers all over America trying to get healed, looking for some man who has the answer. Fear-faith is something that will drive you because of the Fear of death. Fear-faith is a fear that will get you into positive confession, which is a counterfeit for true confession.

It is not what you confess; it is what you *believe in your heart* that you confess. Many people are trying to confess with their tongues, *hoping* it will get into their heart.

Real faith
is when you confess
out of your mouth
what you already believe
in your heart

There are some who say that you just confess the Word of God and He'll honor it. No, God does not honor His Word only because you *confess* it; He honors the Word of God because you *believe* it. "According to your faith, be it unto you."

> **...According to your faith be it unto you.** Matthew 9:29

In your battles against Fear, you must be willing to throw yourself on the absolute care of God. Trust Him whether you live or you die, whether you win or you lose.

Trusting Him does not mean He will immediately remove your problem. If you believe He loves you because He has immediately removed the problem, you have erred. That is fear-faith. When you believe God and trust God, He will set things in motion to lead you out of captivity.

There are a few miracles, but for most people the healing required some time. If God gets involved in your life, He is going to honor His Word to the degree *you* honor His Word. However, there are many people wanting to be healed today who are not interested in serving God. They just want to be well.

There is an exchange that must happen for healing. In exchange for your life, He must become part of it. You cannot get the healing and reject the Healer. Walking out in faith does not mean there is no Fear. You can be in faith, yet Fear will be raging in you just as strong as your faith. The Bible says, "Having done all, stand." Tighten it up one notch and just stand.

> **Wherefore take unto you the whole armour of God, that ye may be able to withstand in the evil day, and having done all, to stand.** Ephesians 6:13

When you are standing in faith while Fear is raging, that does not mean you are in fear-faith; that means you are right in the face of your enemy. It's the best place you can be, because if you are facing the enemy with him raging in your ears, you are still standing in faith. You do not have to cohabit with these spirits.

Do not go black and white in your walk with God. Going black and white is a dangerous mentality, because it will throw you to the far extremes of faith and to the far extremes of Fear. You are not to go to the far extremes of faith, because you have only been given a measure of faith to begin with. But you are not all that Fear represents either. You are somewhere in between.

Let's say Fear is the absoluteness of black in your life, and faith is the absoluteness of white in your life. If you want to diminish the blackness of Fear and its overwhelming reality in your life, you are going to add some light. Take the Word of God and mix it with your faith. The Holy Spirit is there to move and change your darkness into light. You are not alone in this battle. God is with you if you will believe He will meet you.

This is *your* life and God wants you to learn spiritual principles. God wants you to understand this battle because He does not want to have to come back and continually deliver you from Fear. God's perfect will is not to deliver you continually from daily fears. His perfect will for you is that you do not walk in Fear to begin with. You can defeat Fear. Fear is not greater than God! Fear is not greater than faith! Fear is not greater than the Word of God! Fear is not greater than you!

We all need to consider options, not out of Fear, but weighing and considering out of wisdom, according to knowledge. Contingency plans are usually made out of Fear.

Fear will take you into a theology called "the permissive will of God" and get you to settle for second best in your life. Fear reminds you of who you are *not* and what you do not have. Fear reminds you of all the things of your life that are wrong and it projects the same into the future. Fear is excellent in getting you to settle for second best. There is no Fear in the Holy of Holies because that is where the presence of God is and He is not afraid of anything. May we all enter there!

A MEASURE OF TIME

The spirit of Fear cannot be defeated unless the Unloving spirit is defeated first. If you cannot perceive God's love and you cannot love yourself as God loves you, you will never defeat Fear. You must resolve whether you belong to Him or not. There is a measure of time needed for this.

The Bible says,

> **Humble yourselves therefore under the mighty hand of God, that he may exalt you in due time:** 1 Peter 5:6

Many people do not teach there is a season of receiving. I may plant seed in the ground in the spring, but it takes time for it to bear its fruit. The tree may not bring forth fruit until the fall. This teaching is planting seeds so your faith can develop. Your faith, even if it is the size of a mustard seed, sets the Holy Spirit in motion to execute the object of your faith. There are stages of germination and various stages of growth. God knows what it takes to grow you into what you should be.

Fear will tell you that you should be free right now, but you have not germinated yet. You have not grown yet, you have not matured yet and you have not been perfected yet.

You must trust God to grow you up. He wants to! But Fear will not let that happen.

You must expect a measure of time to receive. That really ticks off Fear! Your enemy knows when you believe; he recognizes faith. Then Fear comes demanding, "What about that symptom? Smell this! Do you feel that? God lied to you. If God really loved you, He would deal with you right now." Fear drives. Faith leads.

Faith leads you
Fear drives you

Fear drives you. Fear will come along and act like he is trying to help God and trying to help you get healed. Fear will remind you of your faith but will take away that measure of time to bring forth its fruit, that due season.

Fear will take away the perfecting of God in your life. Fear will demand a fulfillment *right now*. The enemy will send Fear of man, Fear of Rejection and Fear of Failure to deceive you into demanding your healing now. He will coerce you into thinking you should take control of the timing of your healing.

What if you look around in your blessings, in your contentment, in your health, in your wealth, in your peace and your children's happiness and say, "Hey, I did pretty well for myself, didn't I? I am a self-made man, bless God."

God says, "In the day that I bless you, you will forget your captivity and you will forget that it is I who healed you. It is I who delivered you and you will say in your heart, 'It is I who produced my own blessings.' In that day of blessing, you shall leave me again."

> [14]**Then thine heart be lifted up, and thou forget the Lord thy God, which brought thee forth out of the land of Egypt, from the house of bondage;**
>
> [17]**And thou say in thine heart, My power and the might of *mine* hand hath gotten me this wealth.** Deuteronomy 8:14, 17

That blessing shall become your curse. To understand the Old Testament saga of God's people, they go like a roller coaster from blessings to curses as a product of what they determined they would do.

So remember, when you are asking for God's blessings, give Him the glory. Remember what you have been saved from and never exalt yourself in your blessings. You didn't bring the blessing anyway; He did it. God's love for you is reliable. Trust Him.

You can choose to not listen to lies. Fear is a lie. Don't listen to lies. You are going to be surrounded by every evil thing that is in the earth, but you do not have to be a partaker of it. It does not have to rule you.

Knowledge, Instinct and Programming

I was talking to someone recently who said, "I have walked closely with the Lord all my life. How could these horrible things come upon me?"

Things that do not seem right can happen to those who walk closely with the Lord. God, speaking through the prophet Isaiah said, "*My* people"—the people walking closely to Him—"have gone into captivity because they have no knowledge."

> **Therefore my people are gone into captivity, because *they have* no knowledge: and their honourable men *are* famished, and their multitude dried up with thirst.** Isaiah 5:13

Hosea picked up the theme later on. God said again, "*My* people perish because of lack of knowledge."

> **My people are destroyed for lack of knowledge: because thou hast rejected knowledge, I will also reject thee, that thou shalt be no priest to me: seeing thou hast forgotten the law of thy God, I will also forget thy children.** Hosea 4:6

So whether it is no knowledge or lack of knowledge, bad things can happen to good, wonderful people who love God and have walked closely with Him all of their lives. Why? God's people don't know every precept from Genesis to Revelation. They don't know all that is important to their life. They could have missed one of those precepts along the way, opening the door to their problems.

We don't think about Fear of change and Fear of the unknown as being sins which might lead us into captivity or cause us to perish. One of the biggest areas a person with severe allergies, environmental illness, or multiple chemical sensitivities has to face is Fear of coming out of their environmentally safe cocoon. They have Fear because what is on the other side represents change and the unknown.

Now, would you like me to challenge you and thrust you out like a little eaglet that has just come out of the nest and has to fly? This is what the eaglet said, "No, I don't want to go!"

And, what did Momma say? "Get out there."

The eaglet protested, "Yeah, but it's straight down! Do you see the size of these wings? Look at your wings! You have been flying with God for years! But look at me! Look at these scrawny wings of mine!"

I was an eaglet once. I said, "God, You want me to do what? Do You realize how far down it is?"

Do you know what the mother eagle does? She does not ask that eaglet's permission. She does a wonderful, motherly thing. Boom! Suddenly the eaglet finds itself out of the nest and something wonderful happens. It has the ability to fly. It just did not know God had created it to fly.

What met the eaglet in that moment of panic and terror? God showed up in creation.

I did a study on animal instinct versus human, intellectual thought. Here are the nuts and bolts of it. You are different from the animal kingdom because you have to *learn* everything.

It is a scientific fact that humans have to learn everything. They have no instinct, but an animal's brain has been preprogrammed with a "thought impression" that it conforms to and does not know why. That is instinct.

Animals have a brain, too. The Bible says that the only difference between the man and the animal is that when the animal dies, its spirit goes back into the dust, never to exist anymore. The man's spirit returns back to God who gave it.

Your response in how you react to things in your thinking is an established response—what you think is right, what you think is wrong, what you think is up, what you think is down.

You establish what you think is true, what you think is error, what you think is safe, what you think is unsafe. All of this is the product of having been taught at some level, or having been exposed to stimuli at some level and being conditioned in response.

Victimization is being conditioned to be a victim and to be afraid forever. But once you are delivered and free, you can face those same people who hurt you and not run from them anymore. You don't have to be a victim again.

The people who hurt you may never change. They may want to control you and run your life, but you do not have to go down under it anymore, nor do you have the inner turmoil. Your sovereignty as an adult is yours.

PROGRAMMING IN THE WOMB

You may have been programmed by Fear in the womb because your mommy and daddy were full of Fear. They were programmed in the womb too. They spent their whole lives struggling with these forces within. If you want to understand how it is possible for a human to mirror the instinct of an animal, then you have to go from creation to the spirit world.

In creation, God programmed an animal to instinctively know what to do without having to learn from experience. A human has been created by God to learn from experience, so when the person instinctively has Fear, it is something else. There has been a transference of an evil or familiar spirit, right in the womb.

All colicky babies have an inherited spirit of Fear. All gastrointestinal problems, with the exception of Crohn's disease, involve fear, anxiety, and stress. It begins at birth, even if the person is 18, or 28, or 98 before it manifests. We have ministered to many colicky babies and cast out an inherited spirit of Fear, and colic symptoms have left right away. That is ***a more excellent way***™.

Researchers do not know what causes colic in babies. Some say it's the milk. Some say it's something in the mother. Some say it is an antibody. If there is an antibody, Fear is present and you have the reactive reality.

You do not have to be an extension of the curses and failures of your ancestral line. The following testimony gives an example of one journey to freedom from colic.

TESTIMONY OF HEALING FROM COLIC

> My daughter and son-in-law have a child who had colic. When they brought Hannah home from the hospital, she began to have colic all night. They could not sleep. They even put her in a clothes basket on the dryer one night hoping the vibration would make her go to sleep. They were so frustrated.
>
> My son-in-law came to work looking a little bleary eyed from being up all night. He said, "Our daughter has colic."
>
> I said, "Oh, that's easy to deal with. Your daughter has inherited a spirit of Fear. That is the

iniquity of the generations, a familiar spirit, the Fear of Abandonment."

So that night the parents prayed and cast out Fear of Abandonment. The baby slept seven hours.

You know what the good news is? Little Hannah never had colic again. When Tabitha came along, the first thing they did when they brought her home was to set her before the Father by faith and break the power of this iniquity that was traveling in her. Tabitha never had even one bout of colic.

You do not have to conform to your inherited spirituality

Disease Management

Between sanity and Insanity there is a fine line. Between light and darkness there is a fine line. Between love and hate there is a fine line. Between truth and error there is a fine line.

There is a big difference between God and Satan. Satan is always trying to be God; he is always trying to dress up in some spiritual modality to offer himself as the savior of men. That savior, that salvation and that healing bring a different type of bondage, which is lifelong management of the problem.

If you go to a psychologist, he will help you manage the problem. There is no solution for Fear in psychology. You learn to live with it or take a drug to neurologically block the neurotransmitter being deviated by a spirit of Fear.

That is double bondage because you still have the spirit of Fear and you still have the anxiety. It did not go away and you are now tied to its reality which adds other problems. You now have spirits of Sorcery, Pharmakeia and Addiction. They come along to help you live with the Fear and bring all kinds of side effects.

Jesus said,

> **Peace I leave with you, my peace I give unto you: not as the world giveth, give I unto you. Let not your heart be troubled, neither let it be afraid.** John 14:27

Jesus also said, "When the Comforter, the Holy Spirit, has come..." John 15:26 The Comforter is not Prozac.

Prozac
is not a substitute
for the Holy Spirit

A more excellent way™ is not Prozac. ***A more excellent way***™ is the Holy Spirit being our Comforter. Perfect peace belongs to those whose minds, not instincts, are not glued to Fear. Peace belongs to those whose minds are fixed or stayed on the Lord, the Word of God.

When the Word says, "Be anxious for nothing," what are you going to do? What if you inherited the Fear and want to run? God says to stand.

> **Wherefore take unto you the whole armour of God, that ye may be able to withstand in the evil day, and having done all, to stand.** Ephesians 6:13

Did you know Fear of Pain can produce pain? You can also accelerate pain levels by thinking about it. Your body is a responder to your thinking.

Pain is not an emotional or soulish expression, nor is it a spiritual expression. Pain is a physiological expression. Although pain is a physical reality, it can be caused by an evil spirit or by your thoughts.

In the Bible stress is referred to as Fear or "being anxious." We are to "Fear not" and be anxious for nothing. Fear, anxiety and stress are synonymous terms.

Stress and Fear, immediately and in the long-term, directly affect the hypothalamus gland. This is the mind-body connection. Fear, stress and anxiety produce a fight or flight response. Then we have the long-term affects of fear, stress and anxiety in the resistance stage.

Then the hypothalamus says, "Yes, God created them with a spirit of Fear. I am responding to who they are in creation. Body, obey their spiritual realities!"

That is exactly what is happening. Which god are you listening to? Not the God who created you!

Paul said in the letter to Timothy,

> **For God hath not given us the spirit of fear; but of power, and of love, and of a sound mind.** 2 Timothy 1:7

Matthew 6:25 says, "Therefore I say unto you, take no thought for tomorrow." The keyword is "thought," because Fear projected into the future involves thought. Not only is there a spirit of Fear behind it, but you can be programmed to fear. Your body will respond if you cross the parameters of the territorial rights of what that Fear represents.

Fear and stress directly affect nerve impulses. In psychogenic fear, dendrites (nerve cell fibers that receive signals from other cells) flare and pain is the result. This psychogenic pain originating in the mind has no basis in a physical cause.

There are various degrees of pain. If you cut your finger, that pain is organic, not psychogenic, because there is a reason for the pain. Pain can also come from inflammation, as in migraine headaches. There is dilation of the blood vessels in the cranial region coming from the oversecretion of histamine and the undersecretion of serotonin, a vasoconstrictor.

THE MIND-BODY CONNECTION

The hypothalamus-pituitary-adrenal (HPA) chain of command is the brain of the endocrine system, but it is also the facilitator of the mind-body connection. For every thought you have, conscious or unconscious, there is a corresponding chemical, hormone, neurotransmitter, or neuropeptide that secretes somewhere in your body to respond to that thought, trying to maintain homeostasis.

But if there is an aberration because of spiritual problems, we call it "dis-ease." Something that God created to function has now been perverted and it is now malfunctioning most of the time through hyposecretion (under) or hypersecretion (over) of body chemicals.

Much of fear and panic is caused by the hypersecretion of hormones. The amygdala triggers and regulates fear responses and sets the whole fight or flight reaction into motion. When the stressor is gone and the fight or flight reaction consistently extends beyond its normal recovery time due to long-term Fear and anxiety, it carries over into the Resistance Stage.

The Resistance Stage is where you are geared up all the time to face this invisible enemy. Certain parts of your body needed to maintain homeostasis are no longer functioning because your body has been told there is an enemy. So you are geared up, shadowboxing this enemy all this time. After awhile, you wonder why you are worn out.

The third stage is Exhaustion.

FIGHT OR FLIGHT

God created us with fight or flight in its basic stage as part of our creation. But the devil extends it into perversion, long-term, and that's where he "has" us. The devil has programmed us with a fallacy. He is a liar and a deceiver; the name Satan means deceiver. He is a master of deception, manipulation and control.

Even when the danger is gone, you are still geared up for fight or flight. When that happens, your bloodstream is filled with hormones. The beginning of reversing that reaction is when you start to take your peace.

But just because you take your peace and have knowledge does not mean the reaction stops instantly. The evil spirits "have" you again because of ignorance. You believe God, but it doesn't go away instantly.

What happens next? You go right into more fear, unbelief and doubt which accelerate more of the same. If you do not fight this one, the spirit of Fear will control you the rest of your life.

An allergic reaction does not last forever, even when you are *not* fighting it. When you start to take your peace back, you say, "Wait a minute. I have been taught better than this. This does not harm my body."

You can still be having that reaction, that feeling, or that exhaustion, that sickness, that burning or that fuzziness because there are a wide range of manifestations. You can take your peace back in your heart before God that moment, but your bloodstream is still filled with those neurotransmitters. Those upstream secretions are still coursing and it takes a while for your bloodstream to clear.

"Perfect peace belongs to those whose minds are fixed or stayed on the Lord." Isaiah 26:3 All of a sudden you have taken back your peace in your spirit and your soul, but your body is still reacting. Fear is still there; Unbelief is still there.

Take your peace in your mind and in your heart, and your hypothalamus will accept it. Take your peace in your mind and in your heart, and it will affect the peace and health of your body.

You have to remember that God will honor you in your standing and the hypothalamus will shut down the secreting of the hormones. However, the bloodstream is still filled with them. It takes a while for the bloodstream to finish pumping these hormones and the receptor cells to stop reacting to them, until finally the reactions stop and that is the victory.

You have to learn to fight this enemy long-term. You must renew your mind and face the stressor. Eventually, the reaction will not occur anymore because the programming is broken.

That is what happens when people take back their life. One day they are allergic to a hundred different things, and six months down the road they are allergic to none of them. The spiritual dynamics changed and that is the easy part of the freedom. When you are in the situation and in the battle and when you have done all, just stand.

Your problem has a root cause. There is a spiritual bondage: a cause and effect. Some people grasp it faster than others. Sometimes there are things in people's lives that just need to be dealt with before the root can be removed.

There is a battle for your life. This is not mind over matter. This is not a science. This is life. There is an invisible enemy out there that has been controlling mankind for hundreds of years.

Your enemy can be defeated and when he is, God gets the glory. The enemy gets dethroned in the second heaven and we get lifted up above him, and that is to the glory of God. That gives us a place of trusting God and believing in Him. God is greater than evil.

When you are in the battle, sometimes you don't feel very free. When you are in the face of evil, fighting your battle, sometimes you don't know you are victorious until you look around afterwards and say, "Well, I won."

Defeating Fear in Your Life

If your body is being controlled with disease because of Fear, to resolve that issue you are going to have to make new long-term memories. That involves protein synthesis. When you meditate on something from your short-term memory, it goes through a process called protein synthesis which places that memory into your soul, into your genetics. That memory has then become part of your physiology.

Now the true spiritual concept is that God has not given you the spirit of Fear. 2 Timothy 1:7 But you have this new concept counterfeit that says you have been lied to and programmed, and your body is being controlled with disease because of it. How are you going to resolve that issue?

You have to make new long-term memories. Through protein synthesis, your body creates a new unit of memory in your soul. The new unit of memory about what God says is in your soul, so now you have both memories at the same time. You now have the Fear memory and the faith memory.

When you were a child, you thought as a child, but when you became an adult, you put away childish things. 1 Corinthians 13:11 You don't do the same things you used to do as a child, but you remember them. You don't do them now because you have a new unit of memory that represents your adulthood and maturity, although you may feel like doing a childish thing from time to time.

You may think about going back and doing a childish thing because it is still part of your memory, but you subject it to ***a more excellent way***™ of thinking. You need to follow the new thinking although the old one is still there. That is holding every thought in captivity against the knowledge of God. That is your sovereignty and that is your power.

Eventually you will learn to follow the new thought more and more until it becomes a way of life with you. The old thought may be shot back at you as a fiery dart in your moment of weakness and your moment of despair, because it is still there. You do not lose the memory, but the memory can be overcome with a new, ***a more excellent way™***.

When you found yourself ignorant about something, did you continue in the ignorance, or did you immediately develop a new way of thinking to replace that ignorant thought? You may catch yourself remembering that ignorant thought from time to time, but you do not follow it.

When Fear and faith are present together, which one are you going to listen to? If Fear is not your friend, it is your enemy.

The book of Psalms says,

> **21 Do not I hate them, O LORD, that hate thee? and am not I grieved with those that rise up against thee?**
>
> **22 I hate them with perfect hatred: I count them mine enemies.**
> Psalm 139:21-22

HATRED OF EVIL

You are to have a perfect hatred for evil. Fear is evil; it is sin. The perfect hatred for evil is something you will have to ask God to help you develop so you can begin to think the way He thinks.

The two dimensions of Fear include both the spirit and the soul through something called memes, or memories. Your physiological response to Fear can also be on two dimensions. First, Fear comes as the spirit of Fear. Second, it can also come through the programming of your soul by the spirit of Fear, as long-term Fear becomes part of you permanently through long-term memory.

When you have a thought that stays with you for a long time, an electrochemical reaction occurs in the brain. It produces a unit of memory, or a meme: either short-term memory or long-term. If it is in long-term memory, it becomes part of you forever.

Renew Your Mind

In long-term memory there is a mechanism that develops called protein synthesis which is the result of the electrochemical reaction that produces the meme and the locking in of the meme (the unit of memory). Protein synthesis is very important because it involves an RNA component, which is part of your genetic code. Not only do you have the electrochemical impression of your cerebrum, but you now have it locked in as a part of your thinking forever. Fear can become so much a part of you that even if the spirit is removed, you still have some work to do.

Becoming free sometimes requires work. It took you a lot of work to get into bondage, so it may take a little work to get out of it. Not only does the spirit of Fear and everything that it represents have to be dealt with in your life, but you have to renew your mind in faith by making new memes—new units of memory that represent the faith of God for you and what He says about you for the future. Faith takes you into the future.

Fear is not an emotion. Fear is a spirit. But long-term fear can become part of your emotional makeup because that is where your soul is. God has created us to be able to have a godly fear that comes from wisdom.

You don't go out and play in traffic because you know there is a possibility you could get hit by a car. You don't drive on the left side of the road unless you are in England, because you know you would be in a wreck pretty soon. You drive according to wisdom. That wisdom is not the spirit of Fear; it is part of the foundation of understanding good and evil.

You can have a godly fear and a godly understanding so you don't put your hand on a hot stove. You take certain steps to understand the world you live in. You will not play in traffic, but you are not afraid to drive in it because you have wisdom.

There are people who don't want to drive because they have fear of having an accident. Now is that wisdom or Fear? It should awaken you to be more alert to something called defensive driving, which is the result of wisdom, not Fear.

Even though there is a spirit behind Fear, it can create a way of thinking which is not a spirit. You can be so programmed by Fear that you could do the very same thing a spirit of Fear could do and think the very same thing a spirit of Fear could think, without the evil spirit being present. When that happens, you have been "had" because the spirit of Fear does not have to worry about it anymore. He has programmed you and he is very content to make sure he reminds you of what your mind is telling you.

Fear will project the failure of your past into the future. Now Fear is your reality and it has ruined your day.

What does God think about fear? What is His attitude toward it?

Revelation says,

> [7]**He that overcometh shall inherit all things; and I will be his God, and he shall be my son.**
>
> [8]**But the fearful, and unbelieving, and the abominable, and murderers, and whoremongers, and sorcerers, and idolaters, and all liars, shall have their part in the lake which burneth with fire and brimstone: which is the second death.** Revelation 21:7-8

So the fearful will have their part in the lake of fire, which is the second death. Revelation talks about the New Jerusalem, the city that comes down from God, and who lives within and who lives outside.

> **For without *are* dogs, and sorcerers, and whoremongers, and murderers, and idolaters, and whosoever loveth and maketh a lie.** Revelation 22:15

"Outside the gates are dogs" does not mean literal dogs. It means spiritual unbelievers in God. It does not say "fearful" there, but it is included in content and context.

Matthew 6:25 says, "Take no thought for your life, what you shall eat, what you shall drink, or for your body, what you shall put on. Is not life more than meat and the body than clothing?" What is more important to you? What you eat, drink or wear or who you are in life? We are not becoming preoccupied with food, drink and clothing. We should become preoccupied with who God created us to be, which is who we really are. You are created in the image of the living God.

"Behold the fowls of the air. They do not sow." The birds out here are not in fear. I put a little birdhouse outside my place one year. The ducks came to check it out every morning and pick up the birdseed that fell off the little silo when the birds were eating. Some birds sat there and ate, and some sat on little perches. They went through about 50 pounds of birdseed that summer.

Birds are not afraid of what they are going to eat. They do not go out and plant birdseed to eat. They do not plant flowers that have seeds so they can eat. They make no effort to provide food for themselves. "Neither do they reap." They do not go get their own birdseed. They do not gather into barns. They just go find my plastic one. "They do not gather into barns, yet your Heavenly Father feedeth them." Matthew 6:26

Do you think you're a little more important than a bird? You even have been given dominion over all the animals and the birds. If your Heavenly Father looking down makes provision for all the birds on the planet for feeding, do you think He cares for you?

Ignorance is a form of knowledge. If your mind is being renewed, then you are putting into your mind new information from the Word of God and you are mixing it with faith. The author of Hebrews says the same gospel was preached to those coming out of Egypt under Moses and Aaron. The same gospel preached to them is being preached to us today. But it profited them little because they did not mix the Word they heard with faith. They did not believe it.

Mix the Word with faith

Many sick people do not believe in miracles.

> **For unto us was the gospel preached, as well as unto them: but the word preached did not profit them, not being mixed with faith in them that heard *it*.** Hebrews 4:2

Disease is real. It is not a psychological entity, but a spiritual issue with many psychological and biological implications and manifestations. Disease has a myriad of peripheral issues that accumulate long-term.

We can bring a pastoral care program to those who want to partake, even to those who are not healed, even to those who do not believe. We ought to be able to come beside them, encourage them and also educate the church to start being a little more sensitive to their plight.

You do not have to lose this battle between your ears! You do not have to follow pre-conditioned thoughts that represent Fear, because no matter how many physiological manifestations reinforce it, Fear is still a lie.

"Take no thought for tomorrow," and then hold every thought when it does come. You need to be able to grab hold of a negative thought and not be affected, ruled, or controlled by it.

Let's put a measure of time into it. Patience is a good word study. The scripture says,

> **In your patience possess ye your souls.** Luke 21:19

Patience means patient endurance. The soul is right between the ears. Take your peace. Do not be afraid. Even if you are being rejected and maligned by your mother, your father, your brother, your sister, your kinfolk and everyone else, do not let your heart be troubled.

How to Create New Memes

You can remove the protein synthesis within your brain cells that was created by Fear. The antidote is creating new memes based on the Word of God.

When Fear comes, you go first to what the Word says about it, and that's where faith is. That is ***a more excellent way***™. The antidote to Fear is faith and you get that from the Word of God. "Let God be true and every man a liar." Romans 3:4

You may say, "But Pastor, I will be in faith when the Fear is gone."

No. You will be in faith with every roaring spirit of Fear warring in your mind—regardless of your situation. It is time to put your foot down against Fear once and for all. It's time to make Fear your enemy.

If you didn't have the Bible and what God says about fear, if you didn't have the power to overcome it, this really would be a hellacious place to live. You don't have to live with hell as part of your life and your mentality. You have heaven and all it represents at your door!

The Lord's prayer says, "Thy will be done in earth as it is in heaven." Matthew 6:10 There is no Fear in heaven. God is not afraid of anything, nor is He in torment. He is not losing any sleep.

"Well, Pastor, it's so hard."

It is also hard being wiped out by Fear and going through life with all your torment. I want to tell you something. I am a spirit, but I have a soul and I live in a body. Who I am, as a son of God, is a spiritual man.

My spirit does not know disease. My spirit does not know that dimension because disease is a physical dimension. My body can be racked with fever and coughing, and I can feel it in the physical dimension, but what does that have to do with the spiritual man?

It is amazing how your external can control your spirit man and you wonder why. "As a man thinketh in his heart, (in his spirit man), so is he." Proverbs 23:7

The things you are going through have nothing to do with your spiritual capability, or your spiritual position, or who you are in God. I can stand in this earth before the living God and be spiritually correct, regardless of who I am around, and regardless of what I might be going through.

"According to your faith, so be it unto you." Matthew 9:29 I want to encourage you to be a man or woman of God. God says that when we listen to Him, He will be our confidence.

> **And this is the confidence that we have in him, that, if we ask any thing according to his will, he heareth us:** 1 John 5:14

God will be our confidence and will keep us safe from evil. When we truly trust and obey, He will be our protection.

> **Yea, though I walk through the valley of the shadow of death, I will fear no evil: for thou *art* with me; thy rod and thy staff they comfort me.** Psalm 23:4

Types of Fear

There are several types of Fear in God's Word. One is Fear of man. Others would be Fear of evil and Fear of Death.

In the April 2, 2001, issue of *Time Magazine*, there is an article called "Fear Not" which lists over 4,000 different types of fear. The world labels the evil spirit of Fear as "phobias" or "stressors." According to this article, science is offering a new treatment for phobias, which are listed over several pages, alphabetically. Some phobias listed include:

> Fear of mothers-in-law, pastor-phobia, fear of seeing oneself in a mirror, fear of church (ecclesiophobia), fear of crowds, fear of committing the unpardonable sin, fear of marriage, fear of darkness, fear of chickens, fear of man, fear of staying single, fear of spiders, fear of peanut butter sticking to the roof of your mouth, fear of being dirty, fear of germs, fear of cancer, fear of being ridiculed, fear of being touched, fear of cemeteries, fear of constipation, fear of demons, fear of birds, fear of smells, fear of the Pope, fear of flying, fear of punishment, fear of Russians, fear of death or dying, fear of sermons (homilophobia), fear of ridicule, fear of syphilis, fear of dental surgery, fear of animals (zoophobia).

Not only do we see our fears, but also the world sees them. Can I say this differently? Not only do we sin by our fears, but the world also sees our sin. One of our pastors has a saying: "Take your peace." In other words, trust God more.

To fear man is to look to and regard people rather than God. In other words, Fear of man makes man your god. What man thinks and says is what is important to you.

Paul said in Romans,

> **...let God be true, but every man a liar...** Romans 3:4

So if you are going to believe man before God, you are making God a liar and man true.

The book of Proverbs says,

> **The fear of man bringeth a snare: but whoso putteth his trust in the LORD shall be safe.** Proverbs 29:25

This scripture equates fearing man with not trusting in the Lord. One way we fear man in our lives is to hold back from people, worrying about how they are going to treat us rather than looking to God to protect us. There is a close connection between the Unloving spirit and the spirit of Fear.

When you have Rejection and Fear of Rejection, you draw back from people. You do not become transparent with them because you are afraid of Rejection. Who you are depends on what other people think about you.

If you are looking for others' approval, you are in trouble. They think more highly of themselves than they do of you anyway! That is pride and arrogance, the Luciferian spirit.

Fear prevents us from expressing God's love to people. It can lead to us putting more stock in what people think instead of what God says in His Word.

A snare comes if those we fear

are in opposition to God

If you are putting your trust in God, although you still have Fear of man, what will you do if a person full of Unbelief and Doubt comes to you preaching a different gospel? Because you are afraid of him, you could become his disciple. What you are silent against because of Fear, you assent to spiritually and follow.

What you are silent against, you give power to in the spirit. Let's say people who are wrong are coming to you in a gospel of hatred, unbelief, doubt, fear and an antichrist way of thinking. If you are silent because of Fear, you are giving them power.

You are also giving the devil power through them. Sometimes confrontation in love is the best way to go. Just tell them you do not agree.

Why should you listen to the devil speak through someone and you not have the boldness to let God speak through you as the antidote for someone else? Fear would keep you from doing it. You should be able to discuss anything with anyone without fear and without feeling irritated, aggravated, and upset.

A snare could come if those we fear are in opposition to God. We could feel pressured to put their desires above obedience to God. Peer pressure is one very simple example. At the very least, fearing man robs us of the peace God intends for us. It also warps our view of who we are in Jesus Christ, because we take our self-concept from what others think of us, instead of what God says about us in His Word.

That goes back to the Unloving spirit—who you are is what someone else thought about you or said about you. If someone comes to you and says, "Well, I think you're pretty neat," so what? God has already said you are the apple of His eye. Psalm 17:8 You are letting a man be your source rather than letting God be your source.

One antidote for Fear of man is found in the Psalms.

> **The Lord *is* on my side; I will not fear: what can man do unto me?** Psalm 118:6

Another antidote for fear is found in 1 John 4:18. "Perfect love casts out fear." If you do not believe the Lord is on your side, you have an antichrist spirit within you and you need to recognize it. If you do not trust the Lord, who can you trust? Truly trusting in God will remove Fear of man from our lives.

Repent for fearing man. God will transform your heart to trust Him without looking to people as your source anymore. That is a place of peace.

Fear of evil says the devil is greater than God. Fear of evil says evil is able to defeat good every time. Fear of evil says bad things are going to happen to you. Fear of evil projects evil into the future and brings phobic realities.

Fear of evil will always get you to fantasize about destruction. Fantasy always represents the future and is not real. Fantasy can produce a fruit. Fear represents the future, *and* faith represents the future.

Faith *and* Fear are equal in this dimension: they both demand fulfillment, either in actual fulfillment or in tormenting you. Many people are in torment because of what Fear represents, even though it's unfulfilled.

Many fiery darts of Fear of evil come at you in a given day. Many thoughts that are evil represent Fear of tragedy and Fear of things going wrong. You will be bombarded in every facet of your life.

A spirit of Fear will try to get your attention in every dimension of your life—concerning your family, your spouse, your finances and your future.

Many thoughts come and demand that you stop and listen to them. Many of those thoughts come and even produce a feeling from an evil spirit wandering through your spirit looking for a place to roost. So what you say is, "No vacancy! I am filled up! Thank you for stopping, but no thanks."

We need to hold every thought in captivity and cast down every imagination. An imagination can be a phobia, a panic reality, or a fantasy. Phobias, like fear, always involve projection into the future.

PHOBIC IMAGINATION

You are very fertile ground in two dimensions. You are both audio and video in living color. You are an incredible creation with the ability to have auditory and visual playback complete with quadraphonic sound and living Technicolor. In every imagination of your heart you can project onto a big screen in your mind, complete with action and soundtrack.

You are wide open to the billboards of life. You can either pull off to the side of the road or you can keep on driving. When a billboard stares you in the face, it demands your attention. If you keep driving, it's a fading reality.

Is fear on the big screen? Change the channel. You can change your thinking about things. When thoughts come you have a choice. You can find something else to think about, or you can stop and meditate on it.

If you start to hash it and rehash it and munch on it, that thought starts to produce protein synthesis of long-term phobic memory. So getting free of Fear is not just casting out the spirit; your mind must be renewed by the washing of the water of the Word.

The antidote to Fear is what God has said, not what the devil says! Start to believe God instead of the devil.

There is a difference between the spirit of Fear and godly fear. One produces torment and the other produces wisdom for action. All Fear that produces torment is evil. I can be exposed to many things and not be in fear. I can have bad things happening around me and wisdom will take over to solve the problem.

What Job said has encouraged me for years.

> **Though he slay me, yet will I trust in him: but I will maintain mine own ways before him.** Job 13:15

God was not going to slay him. Job came to a place of absolute trust in God. When you trust God, you are not going to fear what man can do unto you. You are not going to have Fear of tomorrow. You are not going to have Fear of death, Fear of dying, Fear of disease. You have to choose to trust God.

Fear comes to plague us all. You feel its presence when it comes. Just because you feel the presence of Fear and what it represents in your life does not mean you have to partake of it. The Bible says that the evil one came to Jesus and found nothing within Him.

> **Hereafter I will not talk much with you: for the prince of this world cometh, and hath nothing in me.** John 14:30

If Jesus had an evil spirit of Fear—which He did not, because He was without sin—He could have yielded to that. It was not fear that took Him to the cross, it was faith.

I believe the Holy Spirit who was with Christ in that dimension of believing is the same Holy Spirit who lives within you and me. I do not believe it was any easier for Jesus than it is for you and me. I believe Jesus came to show us that, as a man, it was and is possible to believe God. Jesus divested Himself of the glory that He had with the Father and He became one of us. The Bible says He was tempted in all points such as we are, yet without sin.

> **For we have not an high priest which cannot be touched with the feeling of our infirmities; but was in all points tempted like as *we are, yet* without sin.** Hebrews 4:15

Fear is a form of temptation designed to steal your faith and to get you to believe what it is saying. You are either going to listen to it, or you are going to put it away.

MANY FEARS

To fear evil is to anticipate or project coming to harm at the hands of evil. If you find yourself on a given day projecting the failure of something into the future, then you have a spirit of Fear demanding that you listen. Fear of evil is to anticipate coming to harm at the hands of evil.

There are many ways we can be in Fear of evil. We can fear exposure to chemicals that we consider evil. We can worry about our lives being negatively affected by people who do not understand or do not care to consider our needs.

We can be afraid of Satan and his kingdom. We can fear personal assault from evildoers.

The Word of God says, "Be not afraid of sudden fear."

> **[25]Be not afraid of sudden fear, neither of the desolation of the wicked, when it cometh.**
>
> **[26]For the LORD shall be thy confidence, and shall keep thy foot from being taken.** Proverbs 3:25-26

Sudden fear is the thing that grips you. Do not fear Fear itself! The scripture does not say "Fear that creeps up on you gradually;" it says "sudden fear." Panic attacks. Phobic attacks. Phobic realities.

Under the word "fear" in the *Merck Manual* it says, "See phobias. See phobic neurosis." It does not say, "See stress." It does not say, "See anxiety." From the medical, clinical observation, fear is called "phobia."

The Word says, "But whoso hearkeneth unto Me (the Word of the Lord), shall dwell safely and shall be quiet from fear of evil." Proverbs 1:33 We can hold onto these words, as they are from the LORD who created the heavens and the earth and all things that are in them. God says that when we *listen to Him,* He will be our confidence and will keep us safe from evil.

There are those who can cause death of our physical bodies. But Jesus said we are not to fear death or those who can harm our physical bodies. He said, "Fear Him that can destroy the body *and* cast your soul into hell fire." Only God can do that. We are not to fear someone who can do physical harm to us.

> **And fear not them which kill the body, but are not able to kill the soul: but rather fear him which is able to destroy both soul and body in hell.** Matthew 10:28

Not only do you go to heaven if you die, but in the resurrection you shall live again forever. That's what it's about. So what is Fear going to do with that? You are so busy hanging onto your life; you have forgotten you are eternal: your eternity is guaranteed in Christ!

Another scripture also deals with this issue.

> **For whosoever will save his life shall lose it: and whosoever will lose his life for my sake shall find it.**
>
> Matthew 16:25

Take no thought for tomorrow, because your Father knows how to take care of you.

Fear of God is sin if it's not holy fear, but negative Fear. If you needed something from me and you were afraid of me, would you come to me? Could you receive anything from me if you were afraid of me? The same thing happens with your Father who is in heaven.

Do you know what happens to us when we are in fear of God? We get in trouble and then we try to avoid Him. We try to work it out behind the scenes without His wisdom.

If you really understood Him, you would go back to the story of the prodigal son. If you ever want to know the heart of the Father, read about the prodigal who took his inheritance, all 14 million dollars of it, blew it and ended up wishing he could at least eat what the pigs were being given because of his hunger.

He decided to return home. When his father saw him coming from a long way off, he did not say, "There is that scurrilous son! I will give him a piece of my mind! I told you this would happen."

No. It says the father saw him coming from a long way off and loved him. He said, "Hey! My son is coming! My son is coming! Fix a party! Fix a big meal!" Before the son even got there, the father was preparing a party.

But his other son said, "Yeah, there's that joker. What's he doing back here?" He was angry in his Jealousy and Bitterness and said, "Well, you didn't do that for me!"

The father said, "Son, everything I have belongs to you now. Everything! And you have been with me always. But he was dead and now he is found. It's party time!"

That is a true story of the heart of your heavenly Father. Fear will not let you go there. Fear doesn't want you to understand the Father.

When you, having blown it so many times, stand before your Father in heaven, the devil will say, "Yeah, you blew it."

Who reminded you of that, the Father or the devil? Don't ever forget God your Father will never condemn you. This is not judgment day. This is a time of grace and mercy. Your Father will accept you.

Jesus said,

> **Come unto me, all *ye* that labour and are heavy laden, and I will give you rest.** Matthew 11:28

All condemnation is of the devil, but all conviction is of God. You have to be able to discern the difference. Your success depends on your discernment.

My definition of conviction is the perception of things that are wrong that need to be changed. That becomes a positive challenge to you because you know you need to change. The Holy Spirit comes to show you change and direction. Change comes out of conviction, knowing you should do something.

For example, if you are driving down the highway on the wrong side of the road because you are looking at that eagle flying up on the side of the road, are you condemned or convicted? You are not condemned. You are convicted. There is a response required that is for the betterment of your life.

God has always convicted me in discernment by turning the lights on, but I do not feel condemned in it because I have the antidote. God said I have fallen short of His glory. He said I would fail. He said I was in the process of being changed. So I know He loves me.

The devil also gives discernment. He reminds me of my failures. That doesn't make me feel good about myself. If I feel bad it is the devil accusing me. If I feel good it is the Holy Spirit convicting me. That is discernment.

So when I feel condemned about myself, I say, "Devil, shut up!" The devil usually accuses you in an area of your life you have not worked out yet. But if the devil is accusing you of something you have worked out, he's coming to see if you are swept clean. He wants to come back into your house, so have your eyes open!

The Holy Spirit does not come to judge. The judgment seat of Christ is not here, not yet, for the saved. So until the judgment seat of Christ comes, we are not guilty.

> **4And I say unto you my friends, Be not afraid of them that kill the body, and after that have no more that they can do.**
>
> **5But I will forewarn you whom ye shall fear: Fear him, which after he hath killed hath power to cast into hell; yea, I say unto you, Fear him.** Luke 12:4-5

The word "fear" here does not mean anything evil; it means "reverential respect." There is something about God that we all need to know.

Luke says,

> **[6]Are not five sparrows sold for two farthings, and not one of them is forgotten before God?**
>
> **[7]But even the very hairs of your head are all numbered. Fear not therefore: ye are of more value than many sparrows.**
>
> **[8]Also I say unto you, Whosoever shall confess me before men, him shall the Son of man also confess before the angels of God:** Luke 12:6-8

The Lord is so concerned about His creation that He notices even a sparrow and the number of hairs on your head. Either you believe that or you don't. If you don't, Fear is your master.

Characteristics of Fear

FEAR IS CONTAGIOUS

There are two characteristics of Fear. First, Fear is contagious. When you are around people who have Fear, you are going to take it on because Fear manifests in a physical dimension, while faith manifests in a spiritual dimension. The physical world demands to control you more than the spirit world. You'll find this out if you get around people who are allergic to food and you're trying to walk out of your own food allergy.

Fear is contagious. Someone yells, "Fire!" The first thing you know, you have a stampede coming out of a mass meme of Fear. People can die, not from the fire, but from being trampled. Looking objectively, it would be a whole lot better just to remain seated.

Moses, in Deuteronomy, recognized this fact.

> **And the officers shall speak further unto the people, and they shall say, What man *is there that is* fearful and fainthearted? let him go and return unto his house, lest his brethren's heart faint as well as his heart.** Deuteronomy 20:8

Not only do you need to be sensitive to the people who are weaker than you, but you also need to surround yourself with people who are stronger than you. Do not be intimidated by people who are stronger. And don't be envious or jealous of them!

We need each other. Do not turn away from others. If someone is weak, they need help. Can you be strong and not be taken down by them? I believe you can.

God is saying watch out for those around you. That does not mean you avoid people who are weaker than you and are full of Fear. It means guard your heart. I know many people who have become strong and will not be around weak people because they think, "I might lose my healing." What is that?

"Well, I just can't stand to be around those people."

How soon we forget!

Jesus is not afraid of our fears. He did not come out of Fear, but out of faith. Here God points out that strong faith encourages some who have been weakened by being around the fearful.

He had those with faith separate from the fearful for the purpose at hand. Before Jesus went to Jarius' house to pray for his dead daughter, He "put out" those who did not believe.

In coming out of Fear, it is wise to have more contact with those who are strong and believing God than with those who could hinder your progress because they are fearful. When you are in your Walk Out, taking your life back, guard your heart concerning those you are around until you get your strength, because Fear is contagious.

Once you are strong, then your faith may be used by God to help those who are still oppressed by Fear. I have seen many people be totally healed by God from their fears, yet they still don't get involved in people's lives because they are afraid they might lose their healing. That is absolute Fear. And that is evil.

Fear can be a self-fulfilling prophecy.

> **For the thing which I greatly feared is come upon me, and that which I was afraid of is come unto me.** Job 3:25

Job said that and it happened just as he said. The thing he feared came upon him.

Fear and faith are equal in this dimension. They both demand fulfillment. They are both spiritual principles. One represents God and one represents the devil, but they both demand fulfillment.

> **Now faith is the substance of things hoped for, the evidence of things not seen.** Hebrews 11:1

Fear is the substance of things *not* hoped for, the evidence *not* yet seen. There is something in the very nature of Fear that brings destruction, rather than life and peace.

Dimensions of Thought

Fear of man, Fear of evil and Fear of Death or disease: these are three big areas you need to get under control. Prepare your heart to be a man or woman of God—whether you feel like it or not. It has nothing to do with feelings.

Your feelings may not even be real. Your thoughts and your feelings may not even be from you. There are voices coming at you from all different angles.

Thought has three dimensions:

- Coming from God as the work of the Holy Spirit
- Coming from you yourself, your own human experience, your own human intellect
- Coming from Satan and his kingdom

All thoughts originate from these three dimensions. You have to discern which dimension you are listening to: God, the devil, or yourself.

If you are listening to God, what you hear has to line up with the Word of God. If you are listening to yourself, what you hear has to line up with the Word of God. If you are listening to the devil, what you hear will not line up with the Word of God.

Paul said to the Corinthians,

> **Casting down imaginations, and every high thing that exalteth itself against the knowledge of God, and bringing into captivity every thought to the obedience of Christ;**
>
> 2 Corinthians 10:5

You are to catch every thought and you are to hold it. One of the greatest victories over Fear is when it is manifesting in you, you stare it right in its face and say, "Okay, I recognize you. Be gone now!"

You say, "That is scary." What is scarier is not resisting these thoughts. When we do not resist them, we become programmed to believe the lies they are telling us.

The basis of all phobic realities is believing lies

Fear of man will keep you from believing God. That is what got King Saul dethroned and caused him to lose his anointing. Through the prophet, God told him to do something. He listened to the people instead and did what they wanted him to do. Instantly, he lost his anointing and his kingship.

> **For rebellion *is as* the sin of witchcraft, and stubbornness *is as* iniquity and idolatry. Because thou hast rejected the word of the LORD, he hath also rejected thee from *being* king.**
> 1 Samuel 15:23

If we find ourselves rebelling against the Word of God—if God says to forgive our neighbor and we do not—then we are guilty of Witchcraft, because the scripture we just read says that witchcraft equals rebellion against God's Word. When God tells you to do something in His Word and you don't do it, then you are stubborn.

Stubbornness is a form of idolatry. Stubbornness makes you a god over God. You say, "God, You are wrong and I am right." Or, "What You said is incorrect and what I have to say about this matter is really the truth."

You have set yourself up over God, against God. You have set yourself in opposition against God and that is the same as if you had become a god. But you are not a god. You are just a piece of created dust that is damned to extinction except for the mercy and grace of the living God.

Apart from general Fear, we also have specific objects that are feared. Fear produces not just a thought, but also a feeling. When you are up against your phobic item or your stressor, you are thinking about it in your head, but you are feeling it in your belly. That is where your spirit man is. You are a spirit. The Holy Spirit also lives within your spirit.

The Word says,

> **...out of his belly shall flow rivers of living water.** John 7:38

If those phobic feelings were just physiological, the only part of your inner organs that would manifest physiologically would be your spinal column; or your heart would be pumping faster through an accelerated flow. There is nothing else in there except the intestines and they do not give off feelings.

An evil spirit communicates with your mind out of the spirit dimension of your life, because it is spirit. An evil spirit is not a human being; it is a disembodied spirit being. It has access to you through your five physical senses in order to program you.

You may not think you have an evil spirit, but we ought not to argue over whether a Christian can have an evil spirit. The question is this: can an evil spirit have a Christian? It does not have you in your mind. It has you in your spirit.

Your spirit and soul have become one in thought, because as God ministers to you from His Spirit, the evil spirit also will want to control you in that dimension.

What you are dealing with in all these projected Fears, whether it be Fear of Death or dying, Fear of man, Fear of losing children or Fear of disease, they are all evil spirits.

An evil spirit is a very intelligent, disembodied entity. It lives within your human spirit, controls you from that place of authority and is able to project thoughts into your soul and into your mind. It is able to control your physiological existence. Your body responds to your soul through the limbic system and the evil spirit controls your soul (your emotions) from the realm of the spirit. The Word also confirms this, which I will prove to you.

Paul said,

> **Put on the whole armour of God...** Ephesians 6:11

Putting on the whole armor is an action God is certainly not going to do for you. It's an action you do for yourself. God does not come down every morning and jerk me out of bed. I have to do it myself. I have to convince myself that I am a man of God and that I am going to act like one. If I fail, I repent. If I get into fear, I deal with it.

> **...that ye may be able to stand against the wiles of the devil.** Ephesians 6:11

"Wiles" is the Greek word, *methodias,* which means method; the means; the plans; the schemes to deceive; to entrap; to enslave; to rule; to bring into captivity. We battle the wiles of the devil.

You may have been taught that God puts sickness and stuff on you to teach you. That is simply not true.

> **For we wrestle not against flesh and blood,** Ephesians 6:12

Our battle is not against humanity or flesh and blood. We are wrestling against principalities and powers. When Fear is coming at you, just say, "No, you cannot! In the name of Jesus, I am going to stand and face you. What are you going to do about that?"

Our battle is not against flesh and blood. Our war is against an invisible kingdom in the earth in the 2nd heaven.

2ND HEAVEN

There is a 1st heaven, a 2nd heaven and a 3rd heaven. The 1st heaven is right here where you and I are. Paul said he was caught up into the 3rd heaven where God is. Three minus one gives us two! If there is a 1st heaven and a 3rd heaven, there must be something in between.

The 2nd heaven is invisible and Satan rules it. He is called the prince of the power of the air. Jesus said, "I saw Satan fall like lightning from heaven." Luke 10:18

The evil one, Satan, was cast out into the earth. Revelation 12:9 Where is he on the earth? The Bible says, "The sons of God came to present themselves before the Lord and Satan came with them." Job 1:6

So the Lord said, "Satan, what have you been up to today?"

Satan answered, "I've been walking up and down throughout the earth."

So where is Satan? He is on the earth. You cannot see him because he is disembodied. He is a ruling principality without a body. No man has seen Satan and no man has seen a literal evil spirit. You have just seen manifestations, because the spirits are invisible.

There is a kingdom that is invisible and that kingdom is real. It needs you to be a medium of expression for itself, because when it cannot manifest, it is in torment. Every evil spirit in a person will manifest at some point.

There are many people in certain churches who teach warfare as if it were a science. Warfare is not a science; warfare is a way of life. Many people teach you how to dress up in the armor and teach you spiritual warfare, but they do not tell you that the only way you can win is if your obedience is fulfilled first.

Obedience First

Many people are trying to be free in warfare that is not working, yet they spend all their Christian life doing warfare. I do not believe in perpetual warfare as a Christian way of Christian life. I believe warfare should lead to freedom; then you do not have that warfare anymore.

How I teach is distinctly different from many others because they teach spiritual warfare as a way of life. I teach it as a way to freedom. I do not believe in perpetual warfare, because I don't think it's a scriptural principle. I believe victory is a scriptural principle.

I think spiritual pride will cause you to get dressed up every morning in your armor. The armor you find in Ephesians 6 is not something you dress up in as a religious rite every morning. It is who you *are* spiritually—no more and no less. You should not have to dress up in it at all. You should go to bed fully dressed in your armor and get up fully dressed in your armor, because that is who you *are*.

Sometimes spiritual warfare is just another form of disease management. It is another form of cohabitation. Jesus said to Satan, "Get behind me, Satan." What does that mean? "Get out of my world. I'm moving on." That is freedom.

I am going on with my life, but not without God and His Word. I need God. I need His Word. I need His presence. I need the Father. I need His Son, the Word. I need the Holy Spirit. I need the Godhead. I need the living God in me every single breath that I take.

So when you tell him "Get behind me," he has already been defeated. He has no more power in that area. When

Jesus said, "Get behind me," He was not concerned if Satan was behind him or not, because He had already defeated him with the Word and He kept on moving.

That armor is frontal for the battle and when you push through your enemy, he is defeated and behind you. You don't have to dress up in this. It is who you *are*. If you are in Christ and you have the mind of Christ, it means you have everything you need.

UNDERSTANDING THE BATTLE

Ephesians says our battle is not against flesh and blood,

> **...but against principalities, against powers, against the rulers of the darkness of this world, against spiritual wickedness in high *places*.** Ephesians 6:12

The battle is not against flesh and blood. That removes humans totally from the battleground. When you are in conflict with people, you think you are in conflict with *them*. No, you are in conflict with the spirits within them that are controlling them and manifesting through them.

If you are not careful, they will be manifesting in you! You will have spirits playing back and forth in a war zone. That's when both of you become victims.

You are wanted as a medium of expression for principalities and powers, rulers of the darkness of this world and spiritual wickedness in high places. You are the prize because, without you, Satan and his kingdom cannot manifest in the physical dimension.

They are caught in a place of torment between heaven and earth. They have no opportunity to physically manifest.

All they have is the thought of the evil with no way to express it. When the evil spirit is within you, it is at rest and you are in torment. When it is gone, it is in torment and you are at peace.

The Word says,

> **Casting down imaginations, and every high thing that exalteth itself against the knowledge of God, and bringing into captivity every thought to the obedience of Christ;**
> 2 Corinthians 10:5

Holding every thought captive, casting it down, holding it, grasping it. Here is where many of the spiritual warfare teachings stop short. They teach you how to do warfare, but they do not teach you how to be obedient to God.

But then verse 6 says,

> **And having in a readiness to revenge all disobedience, when your obedience is fulfilled.** 2 Corinthians 10:6

You cannot have power over the devil in spiritual warfare if your obedience to God's Word is not first fulfilled. It is impossible!

James says,

> **Submit yourselves therefore to God. Resist the devil, and he will flee from you.** James 4:7

You cannot have your good and keep your evil. You must have a readiness to revenge all disobedience. That means you are going to have to develop a perfect hatred for everything that is evil.

If you really hate evil, then why do you allow it to work through you? If you really hate evil, why do you allow it to control your words, your thoughts, your members, your speech, your actions and your deeds? It is because there is a force within you greater than yourself and Paul deals with that in Romans 7.

Fear can be defeated. It can be defeated by truth. It is of the utmost importance to understand that God is greater than the devil. The Holy Spirit is greater than Satan himself and the Holy Spirit is greater than any evil spirit that has ever walked on the face of this earth. You are not alone in defeating Fear. God is with you.

Romans says,

> **...If God *be* for us, who *can be* against us?** Romans 8:31

You are going to have to believe that, whether you want to or not. Your enemy comes along many times in your thoughts and speaks to you as if he were you. He comes along many times as if he were God. He comes along beside you many times with the same thoughts and feelings that any human being would ever have, normally and naturally, but he takes it one step further. He brings into that person's life an aberration of something that was correct.

When the devil creates insanity, he just does not jump into people with a different insane idea and then program them from within. He very delicately distorts the neurotransmitters, serotonin, and norepinephrine. He causes them to hypo-secrete or hyper-secrete. This messes up the neurological transmission of thought and that is what produces insanity. Behind it is an evil spirit of Insanity: the Dumb and Deaf spirit.

Your enemy knows how to control you. It is about time you saw him just as clearly as God in heaven sees him!

You are children of light and not of darkness. God is a good Father and He wants you to know everything He knows about everything. Everything you need to know, He has already written down in the Word.

Obeying God and resisting the devil will produce fruit. Sometimes that happens instantly! Know the truth and the truth will make you free. John 8:32 There is a foundation to this principle. Jesus healed no one or cast out any devils unless He first preached the gospel. That is our ministry model.

Jesus is not here; He is in heaven. He sent the Holy Spirit to represent Him and the Father. He is your Comforter. If you develop that relationship with the Father according to His will in the Word, which is Jesus, the Holy Spirit will be right there to bring you along. That's why I teach the gospel. Know the truth and the truth will make you free.

Then the next thing you must do is submit to God and resist the devil. James 1:5 The devil is not going to flee from you if you are not submitted to God. There are no mantras. There are no mythologies. This is relationship and obedience to the Word of God Who created you for His pleasure.

When all else fails, the third area of ministry is the casting out of evil spirits. Why would we need to cast out an evil spirit? You have already learned the truth by the preaching of the gospel, you have submitted to God and resisted the devil, yet you still are not free.

If Satan has a legal right to your life, we want to find out why. We have to find the open door. We have to find out where those critters came from and why they are still there.

The Sin Within

You are a slave to whatever rules you. Whatever is your master possesses you. Many people misunderstand evil spirit possession. They say Christians cannot be possessed by the devil. I agree because possession, the way they teach it, would be total rulership. And if you are born again, it is not possible for Satan to totally rule your life.

Don't misunderstand the word "possession." Don't go black and white on it.

If you are a beautiful, wonderful Christian who has been born again and who has a heart filled with love and with God—but you cannot control your anger—then in that area of your life, Anger is your master and you are its slave.

That is possession by Anger. That is the area in which you need freedom. That is the area you need deliverance. There are specific areas of bondage and specific types of possession.

Many times in ministry we do know why the evil spirits are still there and we command them to leave in the name of the Lord Jesus. They come back to find out if you have submitted to God, if you believe the Word, if you believe the truth and if it is part of your life.

A lot of people want to be free in Jesus, but they do not want a relationship with God. You cannot have your freedom without having a relationship with God. They are inseparable according to Scripture.

Forgiveness of iniquities and healing of disease go hand-in-hand. You cannot get the healing for your disease if you are not forgiven of your iniquities that caused the disease in the first place.

> **Who forgiveth all thine iniquities; who healeth all thy diseases;** Psalm 103:3

Many people who have spiritual problems in life say, "It's just my flesh." You have just put that battle into the dimension of flesh and blood. "It is just my humanity. It is just my flesh." Ephesians 6 confirmed to us that our battle is not against flesh and blood. It is a battle in the spiritual dimension.

The world is a puppet on a string and God wanted to be the source, but Satan is a manipulator. There are complete nations that are ruled by Satan. There are entire mass memes of control of religion and political government completely masterminded by Satan. There is a master plan for world dominion by Satan.

We have a complete teaching on *Spirit World Realities,* which will help you understand the 2nd heaven. It answers the questions: What is sin? Where did it come from? Where is it now? What is it doing today?

Paul, the great apostle, helps us understand this dilemma in his letter to the Romans. By the time he wrote it, he had been an apostle for probably 15 to 20 years.

This is what he says,

> **For that which I do I allow not: for what I would, that do I not; but what I hate, that do I.** Romans 7:15

That may sound like your life, if you are doing things you hate. Did you ever do anything evil and you knew it was evil when you did it? The more you had the brakes on and said, "I am not going to do this!" the more you did it anyway.

> **If then I do that which I would not, I consent unto the law that *it is* good.** Romans 7:16

That scripture is telling us that when you know to do good but do not do it, you are saying God is a liar. When you do not follow the truth of God's Word, then you are following another law, which is not God's law.

Paul further says,

> **Now then it is no more I that do it, but sin that dwelleth in me.** Romans 7:17

So when I am doing these things which I wish I would not do, it is no longer me doing it, but sin that dwells within me is doing it.

How could Christians have sin dwelling in them? Even if you are born again, that does not mean you are totally free from the control of Satan. Look at the lives of Peter, Judas and David.

It *is* possible for Christians to have sin living within them. That is what Paul was saying. Now then it is no longer I that do it, but sin that dwells where? On the tree next door shooting fiery darts at me, making me do what I am supposed to do through subliminal suggestion? No, Paul really says sin is living *in* him.

> **For I know that in me (that is, in my flesh,) dwelleth no good thing: for to will is present with me; but *how* to perform that which is good I find not.** Romans 7:18

The word "flesh" here does not mean the human body. It means our carnal nature. It is invisible and has to do with an invisible thought.

He says, "in me dwells no good thing: for to will is present with me, but how to perform that which is good I find not." This is pretty typical of human nature. We all want to do good but, the harder we try, the behinder we get. This is warfare. This is reality.

> **For the good that I would I do not: but the evil which I would not, that I do.** Romans 7:19

"But the evil which I would not, that is what I do." Paul said "evil." It is possible for an apostle to do evil. I love Paul for his honesty. What an honest statement by an honest man!

> **Now if I do that I would not, it is no more I that do it, but sin that dwelleth in me.** Romans 7:20

What Paul is saying is that when he does evil, when he does sinful things that are not of God, it is not him doing it, but it is sin that dwells *within* him that is doing it. Paul is saying, "I am doing evil and when I do the evil, then it is not *me* doing it, because the sin that dwells *within* me is doing it."

SIN IS A BEING

Sin is not a thought. Sin is not a state of being. Sin is a being. The Bible talks about the body of sin. Romans 6:6 There is a body of Christ in the earth and a body of sin in the earth. Romans 12:5, 1 Corinthians 12:27

There is a body of Christ here and we are supposed to manifest the full nature of God our Father which is in heaven. There is also a body of sin with many members all manifesting the full nature of Satan. The church is half and half: half manifesting God and half manifesting the devil. By faith you are being transformed and through the work of the Holy Spirit you are being changed.

Fear is not only sin, it is a being itself. When it becomes part of your life, you become a sinful being with it in the area where Fear rules you. But God has not given you the spirit of Fear.

> **For God hath not given us the spirit of fear; but of power, and of love, and of a sound mind.** 2 Timothy 1:7

Paul is saying that he would be doing evil, but it was not even him doing it. When you get into phobias and fears and you dip into the Fear that is manifesting in you, you then find yourself avoiding or not facing that issue. Has that spirit of Fear manifesting in you taken you over?

Now when you have recognized the spirit of Fear that has been gripping you, take your own life back and say,

> No, I am not going to follow that thought or that Fear. I am going to face it. You are a spirit of Fear. Get away from me. I am taking my life back. I am going to face this issue.

So who went into motion there? You did. What was ruling you before? Fear. Who is ruling you now? You are.

God intended that you have full dominion and freedom in this earth in Him. The only way that principalities and powers and evil spirits have access to this planet is with your permission. You give those feelings permission to stay.

You did not know what was in those people who were victimizing you. You did not know it was not *them* hurting you, but it was an evil spirit *in* them manifesting, taking them over. You did not know the evil they did to you was not *them* either. It was a spirit *in* them.

But when you looked at them, you made *them* evil. Paul said in Ephesians 6:12 that the battle is not with *them*. It is with principalities and powers, spiritual wickedness in high places, the rulers of the darkness of this world that is in them, making them do the evil. They are down, it is up and everyone else is a victim.

> **I find then a law, that, when I would do good, evil is present with me.** Romans 7:21

There are two laws in operation through words. There is a *law*, the word of Satan, that's just the opposite of the Word of God. Satan comes to you with his spirit, through people or through your own mind and he writes a law in your heart that is against the law of God.

Fear is a law of Satan to overrule the Word of God. Satan's law says just the opposite so he can get you to follow his word, not the Word of God.

Satan writes laws and rules and regulations and he writes a law in your heart that does not agree with the law of God. The Bible says you are to write the law of God in your heart, upon the tables of your heart. That is the renewing of your mind by the washing of the water of the Word.

> 12**For the word of God *is* quick, and powerful, and sharper than any twoedged sword, piercing even to the dividing asunder of soul and spirit, and of the joints and marrow, and *is* a discerner of the thoughts and intents of the heart.**
>
> 13**Neither is there any creature that is not manifest in his sight: but all things *are* naked and opened unto the eyes of him with whom we have to do.** Hebrews 4:12-13

Fear is an evil spirit, not an emotion. The Fear you are dealing with is not an emotion, but it will produce an emotion. It will produce a feeling. It will produce physiological realities, but behind this is an evil spirit of Fear.

Not only is it a spirit, but it can program your thinking, your memes and your long-term memory through protein synthesis, so that you now have become one with Fear, not only in spirit, but also in soul.

The Word of God comes to separate the soul from the spirit by bringing in the Word of God to wipe out that bonding of soul and spirit where you became one with an evil spirit. Get that thing separated so it can be defeated!

Biblical Evidence for Evil Spirits

Let's talk about Uncle Job. He had thoughts from the visions of the night and Fear came upon him—sudden Fear and trembling that made his bones shake.

> **13In thoughts from the visions of the night, when deep sleep falleth on men,**
>
> **14Fear came upon me, and trembling, which made all my bones to shake.** Job 4:13-14

This describes the mind-body connection. The Word does not call it that because technology and science and understanding had not arrived yet, but God knew what He was talking about.

Job was a contemporary of Abraham. The Book of Job is the oldest book in the Bible and it was written before the law was ever given. Job did not even have the law, did not have the Word, did not have anything. He just had a relationship with God. He did not have it according to full knowledge either, because the law had not been given yet.

What happened to him was a panic attack, or an anxiety attack. This is pretty excessive fear.

> **15Then a spirit passed before my face; the hair of my flesh stood up:**
>
> **16It stood still, but I could not discern the form thereof: an image *was* before mine eyes, *there was* silence, and I heard a voice, *saying,*** Job 4:15-16

An evil spirit appeared to Job. The Old Testament is very silent on the issue of evil spirits because there was no provision made to defeat them except through sheer obedience. God wanted His people to obey Him regardless of the devil, just because they wanted to.

Sheer obedience is what the law brought and it didn't work because the people didn't want to serve God. Today we have grace and mercy and through Christ we have more understanding about this kingdom in Matthew, Mark, Luke, John, Ephesians and other books of the Bible.

Why isn't there more said about evil spirits in the New Testament? It is because that wasn't God's emphasis. The emphasis was on relationship with Him and your nature being changed, not the overemphasis of Satan and his kingdom. But there is enough information to show you where this stuff comes from. Many people say, "Well, I don't deal with evil spirits because that passed away with Matthew, Mark, Luke and John."

Well, what about Ephesians 6? It didn't pass away, did it?

What about Romans 7? Paul was saying he had sin that dwelt within him. What are you going to do with that?

It is a New Testament principle. Now, not only did Paul call Fear a spirit in 2 Timothy 1:7—not only did he say the battle is not with ourselves personally, but with principalities and powers, spiritual wickedness in high places, rulers of the darkness of this world—but all the way back to Job, Fear is associated with what? An evil spirit and a spirit of trembling and anxiety.

Defeating Fear with Scripture

The answer to Fear can be found in the Word. Psalm 91 is a great scripture against Fear.

> **He that dwelleth in the secret place of the most High shall abide under the shadow of the Almighty.** Psalm 91:1

That has to do with a relationship with the Godhead. "He that dwelleth in the secret place..."

> **2I will say of the LORD, *He is* my refuge and my fortress: my God; in him will I trust.**
>
> **3Surely he shall deliver thee from the snare of the fowler, *and* from the noisome pestilence.** Psalm 91:2-3

A fowler in the old days used to set traps for birds; the snare was used to catch the bird. The guy who set the trap was called the fowler. He shall deliver you from the entrapment that the devil has planned for your destruction and bondage.

> **He shall cover thee with his feathers, and under his wings shalt thou trust: his truth *shall be thy* shield and buckler.**
> Psalm 91:4

That matches up with the armor of Ephesians 6:12. His truth is His Word and it shall be thy shield and thy buckler.

> **5Thou shalt not be afraid for the terror by night; *nor* for the arrow *that* flieth by day;**
>
> **6*Nor* for the pestilence *that* walketh in darkness; *nor* for the destruction *that* wasteth at noonday.** Psalm 91:5-6

"Thou shalt not be afraid for the terror by night. Nor for the arrow that flieth by day. Nor for the pestilence that walketh in darkness." That would be Fear of disease. "Nor for the destruction that wasteth at noonday." That could be

Fear of destruction, Fear of losing your life, Fear of lost life. Here is a provision for taking care of Fear and torment.

There are so many of God's people today in the New Testament church who are afraid. Separation from God makes you a sinner in fear because when you accept Fear, you do not trust Him anymore. You trust your Fear more than you trust what God has said.

Trust God more than you trust Fear

So what happens when you say you love God, yet you do not? What happens when you say you trust God, yet you really do not? Does that make you a hypocrite? What comes when you say you trust God, but you do not? Fearfulness.

The root of all Fear is not trusting God. Fear is an antichrist spirit because it casts down what God has said about His faithfulness to you. It is your choice whether you would rather believe a lie than believe the truth.

But because you would rather believe a lie than believe the truth, God says He will give you over to greater delusions. 2 Thessalonians 2:11 You will go into a spirit of panic and from panic to phobias. You are then in more and more captivity because you would rather believe a lie than believe the truth.

Like begets like. Fear begets Fear. Once you allow Fear to become part of your life, what comes down the road is just more of the same. There are corresponding physiological (physical) problems that come out of it.

In the Torah was a scripture for all good law-abiding Jews and all rebel Gentiles.

Deuteronomy says,

> [58]If thou wilt not observe to do all the words of this law that are written in this book, that thou mayest fear this glorious and fearful name, THE LORD THY GOD;
>
> [59]Then the LORD will make thy plagues wonderful, and the plagues of thy seed, *even* great plagues, and of long continuance, and sore sicknesses, and of long continuance.
>
> [60]Moreover he will bring upon thee all the diseases of Egypt, which thou wast afraid of; and they shall cleave unto thee. Deuteronomy 28:58-60

This lack of observing the law spells out the basis for Fear of disease.

> [61]Also every sickness, and every plague, which *is* not written in the book of this law, them will the LORD bring upon thee, until thou be destroyed.
>
> [62]And ye shall be left few in number, whereas ye were as the stars of heaven for multitude; because thou wouldest not obey the voice of the LORD thy God. Deuteronomy 28:61-62

"And they shall cleave unto you… every sickness… because you would not obey…"

What is the key? "You would not obey the voice of the LORD thy God."

So if you were told to forgive your neighbor, what would you do in your disobedience? You would hate your neighbor.

If it says not to fear, what would you do in your disobedience? You would fear. If it says to trust God, what would you do? You would not trust God. If it says not to trust in man, what would you do? You would put your trust in men.

> [63]And it shall come to pass, *that* as the LORD rejoiced over you to do you good, and to multiply you; so the LORD will rejoice over you to destroy you, and to bring you to

> **nought; and ye shall be plucked from off the land whither thou goest to possess it.**
>
> **64And the LORD shall scatter thee among all people, from the one end of the earth even unto the other; and there thou shalt serve other gods, which neither thou nor thy fathers have known, *even* wood and stone.**
>
> **65And among these nations shalt thou find no ease, neither shall the sole of thy foot have rest: but the LORD shall give thee there a trembling heart, and failing of eyes, and sorrow of mind:** Deuteronomy 28:63-65

"A trembling heart" is severe anxiety. "Failing of eyes and sorrow of mind" is depression.

> **66And thy life shall hang in doubt before thee; and thou shalt fear day and night, and shalt have none assurance of thy life:**
>
> **67In the morning thou shalt say, Would God it were even! and at even thou shalt say, Would God it were morning! for the fear of thine heart wherewith thou shalt fear, and for the sight of thine eyes which thou shalt see.** Deuteronomy 28:66-67

"And your life shall hang in doubt before thee. And you shall fear day and night. And you shall have none assurance of your life." That is Fear of losing your life, Fear of Fear, Fear of disease, Fear of Death, Fear of dying.

"In the morning you shall say, 'I wish to God it were evening.'" When you get up, you just do not want to go through your day.

"Then at evening you shall say, 'I wish to God it were morning.'" Why? "For the fear of thy heart wherewith thou shalt fear and for the sight of thine eyes which thou shall see." What you see and feel with your five physical senses can bring you fear.

Mark 7 and Matthew 15 also tell us where evil comes from. The scribes and the Pharisees came, saying, "Wash your hands before eating."

Jesus said it's not what goes in your mouth that you eat with unwashed hands that defiles a man. Jesus explained that whatever comes from outside a man goes in his stomach only, not into his heart and it therefore cannot defile him.

> **11Not that which goeth into the mouth defileth a man; but that which cometh out of the mouth, this defileth a man.**
>
> **16And Jesus said, Are ye also yet without understanding?**
>
> **17Do not ye yet understand, that whatsoever entereth in at the mouth goeth into the belly, and is cast out into the draught?**
>
> **18But those things which proceed out of the mouth come forth from the heart; and they defile the man.**
>
> **20These are *the things* which defile a man: but to eat with unwashen hands defileth not a man.** Matthew 15:11,16-18,20

He said, "That which comes out of the heart of man is what defiles the man." This also corresponds with what Paul said in Romans 7. This is an extremely important principle. It helps you separate yourself from that kingdom within which you do not want to be one with.

God has not created you to be fearful. Fear is within you and it is manifesting itself by its nature, controlling your mind and eventually putting all kinds of diseases into your body that are called fear-stress diseases. Many of the diseases we deal with are the result of fear, anxiety and stress.

Fear and disease go hand-in-hand. It's a high price to pay for agreeing with Fear.

"From within, out of the heart of man proceed evil thoughts." The definition of the word "fear" in the Old Testament from the *Strong's Concordance* says that it is an emotion, a feeling.

What are feelings? These are the feelings you have down in your belly. You have thoughts in your mind, but you feel them down in your belly. That happens when you have become one with a spirit. Your soul and your spiritual dimension have become one.

What needs to be separated? Your soul and your spirit. They can be separated from becoming one in that evil area of bondage in your life.

You need to be able to recognize it is not you and that it has to go. Fall out of agreement with it. Everything that is not good for you is from the devil. It needs to go. You have a choice to make. Are you going to cohabit with it or command it to go?

Out of the heart of man proceed evil thoughts: adultery, fornication, murders, thefts, covetousness, wickedness, deceit, lasciviousness, the evil eye, pride. All these evil things come from within and defile the man.

> **18But those things which proceed out of the mouth come forth from the heart; and they defile the man.**
>
> **19For out of the heart proceed evil thoughts, murders, adulteries, fornications, thefts, false witness, blasphemies:**
>
> Matthew 15:18-19

Jesus is not talking to some unsaved, unregenerated Gentiles here. He is talking to members of the Old Testament church who had become separated from Him and His Word. The Bible was not written to the unsaved. It was written about God's people, accepting their failure and making a provision for the unsaved.

The Old and New Testaments were written about God's people, to God's people, with a provision for all of mankind through Jesus Christ. That is the bottom line.

Now you cannot get off the hook, Christian, because you have evil. Do not negate grace and mercy. This is discernment. This is sanctification and holiness and renewal so that from glory to glory we can be changed, and not stay in bondage to the evil one.

Roots of Diseases and Conditions

ACNE

This disorder is usually on the face, neck, back and shoulders. Medical research has identified adolescent acne as fear, anxiety and stress that is a result of peer pressure. Kids are afraid of other kids. This triggers increased histamine secretion behind the skin and also increases the secretion of oil in the epidermis.

ALLERGIC REACTIONS

In allergic reactions, when a person comes in contact with their stressor or forbidden item, their heart starts to race. They are exposed to the stressor and it begins to growl, "I am here. What you going to do with me?"

"Oh, no!"

The mind remembers the previous reactions. The mind may even remember anaphylaxis. It may remember catatonia, brain fog, prickling of skin, pain, blotches and burning of the skin. It may remember fatigue.

All of a sudden you are being bombarded with what that stressor represents physiologically. Your respiratory rate increases (pant, pant, pant, pant). The cardiac muscles start to expand and contract, and breathing becomes more difficult (pant, pant).

Then you go from fear into the panic stage and start to breathe harder and harder. Finally you start to lose your breath and look for your oxygen because you cannot get your breath.

But what your enemy—or your doctor—has not told you is that you have just stepped into something called hyperventilation, which causes the rapid breathing. You are not even aware of it because you are so preoccupied with your stressor and the fear of it. More Fear comes in because like begets like.

Now you are surrounded by this reality. The carbon dioxide in your lungs is not being exhaled like it needs to be, and the oxygen is not getting into your lungs. That's what happens in hyperventilation. Next comes low-grade carbon dioxide poisoning or oxygen starvation.

When the bloodstream picks up the blood in your lungs, it goes to pick up the oxygen, but there is none. The first part of the body to receive oxygen is the brain.

The brain says, "Get the first bit of oxygen," but there is no oxygen. When you do not have oxygen for your brain cells, you have fuzziness of thinking and disorientation. You feel confused. You feel like you are losing your mind. You feel like you are going crazy. You cannot think right and you start to lose it. You feel faint and think you are going to pass out. You are looking for oxygen, but all of a sudden panic is here. That is an allergic reaction. Finally when you get the oxygen turned on, you take a breath because then you can breathe.

But what took your oxygen away from you in the first place? Fear.

Fear is a triggering force in the mind-body connection. When that spirit of Fear (or what Fear has put into your mind long-term) sets into motion a wide range of neurological and hormonal reactions, then it is fight or flight.

What's more, environmental allergic reactions can be created by the power of suggestion. I had a lady with EMF (electromagnetic field sensitivity) tell me a few years ago that while she was in her back bedroom, someone came in the front door and turned on a 20-watt light bulb in the kitchen and she had a reaction.

She said, "I did not know anyone came in the house and I went into reaction immediately. Now tell me that is the power of suggestion."

I said, "You misunderstand something. You have a living, invisible entity that is in you that can see through walls and doors. It knew when someone walked in. It knew exactly how to program you for the future in that area."

She was shocked to find an evil spirit could see through walls and doors or that it would know how to trigger a reaction to reinforce its position in her life.

This lady is well today and no longer has electromagnetic field sensitivities, because once the broken heart is healed, the immune system begins to heal. When the immune system begins to heal, allergies fall off. If the allergies are rooted in extreme phobic realities, they fall off even before the immune system is healed because when the person understands the concept of phobic reality, the lights go on and the jig is up.

ALLERGIES

Fear compromises the immune system and instructs the body's chemistry to secrete hormones and neurotransmitters, which long-term brings destruction of killer cells. Because the immune system is compromised, B cell antigens kick in as the result of the mind-body connection and you have allergies.

All allergies, without exception, are rooted in a spirit of Fear. With a strong immune system, there is no allergy; with a weak immune system, there are many. Allergies and a compromised immune system go hand-in-hand.

If I am allergic to something, I have Fear and stress. If I am no longer allergic to it, I have changed; the Fear and stress are gone.

You can react to anything. I can create an allergic reaction in you by my words. If I can get an allergic reaction by my spoken word, an invisible entity can do it by planting the thought within you. Your enemy is an intelligent being and he can set that into motion just like he did with the lady with EMF.

ANXIETY DISORDERS

Phobias appear to be associated with an increased family history of anxiety disorders and the anxiety itself is often a fearful reaction expressed in excessive activity of the autonomic nervous system. Physiologically, anxiety begins in thought, but it expresses itself through the nervous system and the endocrine system.

This physical expression is not through neurological impulses but through chemicals that are being manufactured by your hypothalamus gland. Even when you are delivered from an evil spirit of Fear, you still need to have your mind renewed by the practical application of walking out of it—walking away from it. You have to face your fears.

ASTHMA

Asthma is a fear-anxiety disorder. In fact, Johns Hopkins University, after months of research, determined that a person having an asthmatic reaction or attack was not reacting to anything external. No allergies, no pollens, no irritants; nothing!

Nothing external was causing an asthma attack. It was something internal causing the stiffening of the alveoli. They have proved it conclusively, and the conventional wisdom on asthma for the past 50 years has been changed.

Asthma is the outcome of cell membrane semi-rigidity caused by fear, stress and anxiety. It is not biological; it is not genetic. It is caused by familiar spirits that were inherited. There is a spirit of Fear that came into the child from birth.

Blood Clots

When a blood clot tears into the artery you have a component of Fear plus Rage and Anger. Rage and Anger are also behind strokes, aneurysms, varicose veins, hemorrhoids and anything that involves a clotting or an explosion of blood vessels in areas where we do not find high cholesterol levels.

Cancer

Cancer can be a virus. Chemotherapy does not destroy the virus; it destroys the mutated cells in which the viruses reside. Cancer is a genetic, physiological parasite. It takes the RNA and the DNA from your cells and uses it to mutate into its own genetic composition.

Cancer is highly demonic because it indicates an intelligence behind the scenes. Bacteria do not have an intelligence that causes them to do anything. They are just there. A virus has a type of intelligence which has a design behind it and it knows exactly what it's doing.

ENVIRONMENTAL ILLNESS

People have been able to take things back because they now know the truth, not just because their immune system was healed. They were having phony environmental illness (EI) reactions and did not even have an allergy to begin with. They had an EI reaction based on Fear.

There are two dimensions to environmental disease. One is because of real allergies that come from a compromised immune system and the other is pseudo allergies which come out of a fear-anxiety reaction. Long-term, the pseudo allergies will affect your immune system too, because all fear breaks down your immune system.

You can have a mirrored allergic reaction and not be allergic to the product whatsoever. A phobic reality is your reaction to something that is a forbidden stimulus. It is on your list of stressors.

FATIGUE AND LETHARGY

This is found under the third stage of the General Adaptation Syndrome and is called exhaustion. Many medical manuals attribute fatigue and lethargy to fear, anxiety and stress.

FRIGIDITY AND IMPOTENCE

Conditions such as frigidity and impotence are also a biological fruit because they are rooted in anxiety and fear.

HEART ATTACKS

The heart muscle is the first receptor for the docking of the hormone sent out by the hypothalamus in conjunction with Fear. The Bible says in the last days men's hearts will fail them for Fear. That's a big revelation. God said it three thousand years ago!

> **Men's hearts failing them for fear, and for looking after those things which are coming on the earth: for the powers of heaven shall be shaken.** Luke 21:26

Many heart diseases, heart problems and angina are rooted in fear and anxiety disorders. In angina there is a stiffening of the heart muscle to the degree that it calcifies the heart, not allowing flexibility for the heart to be able to pump like it needs to.

Fear will always strip you of your faith. I talked to an individual in another state who is a pastor. He just had a heart attack, which is a genetically inherited problem. His dad had a heart attack at the very same age he had his. Then his dad had another one several years later that required a heart bypass.

Do you think we need to prevent another heart bypass in about six or seven years? We are going for it! Disease prevention is as important as disease healing. It would be important for that pastor not to have another heart attack in his life.

HIGH CHOLESTEROL

Cholesterol levels have nothing to do with the root issue behind heart attacks. Heart attacks can be the result of an artery that has closed because of high cholesterol. When we get into the study of cholesterol and triglyceride levels in excess of 300 as a long-term rating, then we have two separate classes of people: the ones who have plaque in the arteries and veins and those who do not.

What is the difference between these two groups? There is a spiritual reason; there is a spiritual problem. In the case of these high levels, we find that there is a history of long-term Bitterness, Anger and Rage.

So if you want to prevent some of these diseases, you have to get the root of Bitterness out; you have to get out of Rage and Anger so you can live.

HIV AND AIDS

A virus, such as HIV, has such intelligence behind it that when it is confronted it will cross-mutate. It will develop a whole new mutation to avoid contact with any invader. HIV has mutated into thousands of different forms.

Science has tried to develop a drug for HIV, but when the virus is confronted with a drug, it mutates to avoid the conflict. So you can design the drug, but all of a sudden what you are after isn't there anymore. It has mutated.

Mutation changes the mold. In order to make a coin, someone creates a mold from liquid copper. When it hardens, they pour liquid nickel into the mold, let it solidify and stamp out the coin. This becomes an exact copy of the original.

Viruses such as HIV mutate the genetics of the host to create another genetic form. That mutation is now the original, kicking out nickels just like the mold of itself.

If the virus is confronted, it stops, takes the host's genetics again and re-mutates. Now, instead of having a nickel, we have a quarter. The quarter now starts stamping out other quarters fashioned just like itself.

When the quarters are confronted, they sense the confrontation, mutate and then make a new mold. Now we have another new virus—this time just like a penny. It's that fast.

AIDS is the breaking down of the immune system because of the HIV virus attacking the cells while the person is defenseless. AIDS is not the real disease. AIDS is a fruit of disease, which is the HIV virus. So to have a healing, the HIV virus must no longer exist in any mutated form. And the only true healing of HIV is when testing proves that. I am interested in the destruction of the HIV virus by God!

INCONTINENCE

Many times incontinence may also be found in fear, anxiety and stress disorders.

INSOMNIA

The hypothalamus gland regulates sleep, so if this gland senses conflict or fear, anxiety and stress, it responds and interferes with the peace of this person.

MIGRAINES

The psychogenic pain of migraines produces real pain, which is caused by conflict with oneself out of a combination of Fear and Self-Hatred. The conflict causes an under-secretion of serotonin and an over-secretion of histamine. If you will get out of the spirit of Fear and get rid of the spirits of Self-Rejection, Self-Hatred and Guilt, you will overcome migraine headaches.

OVEREATING

Overeating is a false comforter. Four powerful forces drive this, producing long-term fear, anxiety and stress. They are Fear of Rejection, Fear of man, Fear of Failure and Fear of Abandonment.

A person who is driven burns large amounts of fuel supply which produces a chemical need for nutrition replacement beyond the normal.

PHOBIAS

In many respects, the etiology of phobias is similar to that of neurotic anxiety and general phobias appear to be associated with an increased family history of anxiety disorders. When I find Fear and anxiety, I look at the family tree. The problem is often generational and inherited.

If it is inherited there also may be a biological issue, because there is a defective gene. Genes are not soul or spirit; genes are part of your physio (your physical body); a defect can be in the brain cells. Your soul is where the brain cells are, but your spirit is in the inner man.

So you have a biological defect in an area of the soul that affects your ability to think. You are very mechanical in thought—the processing of mixing and matching pieces or units. Computers are fashioned like you are, with your units of memory.

VIRUSES

There is something within Fear that has the ability to integrate units of memory and we would call that a virus. It does the same thing in us that it does in the computer system. It prohibits bringing memory back the way it is supposed to be.

Within you, a virus interferes with biological processes. The medical community calls a virus "an alien life form." It is an alien life force because it takes the components of life, biologically, from an amino acid base. It is genetically aberrated in a way that is not common to the way it is in creation.

A virus duplicates itself after the genetics that a human does in cell replication, DNA and RNA. A virus has genetic life and replicates itself according to a genetic code, but that genetic code is not normal to creation. It is an aberration of creation that produces disease in your life.

All viruses
are evil spirits of Infirmity

In dealing with a virus, we command its genetics to be changed and eliminated so it does not exist anymore. We command it to die and command the white cells to attack it. Bacteria can be destroyed with antibiotics, but a virus cannot be destroyed by any medicine known to man.

Viruses can be diverted, interfered with, redirected, blocked or expelled, but not destroyed. The white cells attack them and expel them as a waste by-product. They are an alien life force.

MECHANISMS OF THE SPIRIT OF FEAR

You need to renew your mind by the practical application of walking out of your fears—walking away from them. You have to face your fears. However, further psychological mechanisms are projection and displacement. Some of these psychological mechanisms include soul, mindset, memes, units of memory, emotions, programming of thoughts and placement of perception reinforced by evil spirits.

The *Merck Manual* calls projection and displacement psychological (soul) manifestations. Displacement means avoidance. That is how you are programmed. It is the work of the spirit of Fear.

You have an unpleasant physiological (physical) reaction and you know something is not good for you. Before you even avoid it, you *project* avoidance (by your thoughts). In extreme phobias a person's entire day from waking to sleeping—even in the middle of the night—projects the failure of the next day.

It is now no longer just projection and displacement; it has become a way of thinking. Spiritually and psychologically (in spirit and soul) you have become one with what Fear represents. Physiologically your body will respond to the hypothalamus, agree with it and pitch a fit.

CELL MEMBRANE PERMEABILITY

A component of Fear and anxiety, long-term, is cell membrane permeability and cell membrane semi-rigidity.

Why do certain people retain toxins and others do not? We can be exposed to certain chemicals and toxins in huge quantities that could affect us genetically more than it would harm us in any other area. There are exceptions, however, because chemical injury can be devastating. In some diseases, the types of toxins that are retained would be coming out of normal lifestyles.

So why do certain people retain toxins while others do not? God created the body to cleanse itself. He gave us an immune system to attack invaders. He gave our body the ability to cleanse itself through the process of osmosis, which is the back-and-forth free flowing of the fluids in the cells. This is called cleansing. Mark says, "If you drink any deadly thing it shall not harm you."

> **They shall take up serpents; and if they drink any deadly thing, it shall not hurt them...** Mark 16:18

We do not use that as a form of tempting God and go out and drink PCBs just to make sure that scripture works. That is tempting God and you could die. But if you are exposed to something in normal, everyday life, there should be a protection for you if you believe. If you do not believe, there is none.

TOXIC RETENTION

Fear and anxiety can produce a number of cell membrane semi-rigidity diseases. One is asthma. Another is hypertension or high blood pressure. Another is the retention of toxins because of cell membrane semi-rigidity.

That is why you may end up with a high toxicity level and get into alternative modalities of cleansing. Toxic retention occurs because of cell membrane semi-rigidity, which comes from Fear. The same dynamics produce asthma, hypertension and vasoconstriction. These are the fruits of long-term thoughts of Fear and anxiety.

Remember that phobias are Fear or anxiety. The physiological manifestation in the body begins in the soul. From a spiritual standpoint, we know that it begins in the realm of the spirit.

ASSOCIATIVE REACTIONS

Projection and displacement focus the anxiety on specific external objects or situations. When you are into fear and anxiety, there is an object of focus in your life. Sometimes you are actually thinking about it. Other times it is there beyond the realm of conscious thought. That is what causes the Resistance Stage of the General Adaptation Syndrome of Fear, Anxiety and Stress.

Further psychological mechanisms, called projection and displacement or avoidance, focus the anxiety on a specific external object or situation. It then comes to represent the underlying original source of the anxiety. There is an *association.*

The physiological manifestation of anxiety and panic is now associated with something very specific. For example, you know that perfume is what causes you to react. You know it because, when you are around perfume, you have a reaction.

You come to associate the perfume with the reaction and from a phobic standpoint you know there is something in that perfume that is not good for you. You have just been programmed to believe the biggest lie of your life.

You are reacting to perfume because your immune system was broken a long time ago, through the long-term work of Fear and anxiety. When your immune system is broken, your B cells are compromised and you have an antigen-antibody mechanism that goes into motion immediately.

You could be allergic to one thing or a thousand different things! Allergies begin with a compromised immune system. The medical community knows that fear, stress and physiology show the progression of cortisol and the catecholamines and how they compromise and destroy the B cells of the marrow of the bone.

The Antigen-Antibody Connection

However, researchers could find an antigen-antibody connection in asthma. So a person with that disease could actually have a real allergy, because of a compromised immune system. In this Johns Hopkins study, they were finding that most people with EI did not react on the IgE RAST test for allergies. And because they didn't show up as regular allergies, that's one reason they had so much trouble getting insurance coverage.

There was one lady who had both regular allergies and pseudo allergies and they all healed at the same time. She had the regular IgE antibodies lab test, with its documentation of two allergies and the pseudo-phobic allergies. So there could be a combination of both types of allergies present.

People have said, "Well, they really didn't have allergies to begin with." In our documented cases of people that have been healed, the IgE lab test is given to prove they had real allergies.

Whether they did or they didn't, a reaction is a reaction. You are susceptible to thought. You are susceptible to be programmed to Fear and that is why your mind needs renewing by the washing of the Word.

You have a very real enemy, an evil spirit, who can use a 20 watt light bulb to create a reaction in a woman with EMF. If we have an invisible enemy who is that intelligent, what else can he do to you? How else can he make you sick? Do you know how fast a spirit of Fear can irritate the lining of your stomach and your intestines to give you gastrointestinal problems?

Do you know how expert your enemy is at working you over? I think it's time for him to be x-rayed in discernment and brought from the invisible into the visible. The only way we can really discern the invisible is by seeing the fruit of it.

FACING YOUR STRESSOR

But it takes some work to get this into your heart and get you to a place where you can be free. This is where you take this knowledge and mix it with your faith. That truth will make you free.

What do you find yourself doing with something you are fearful of? The Word teaches you to walk right up to your enemy and say, "How are you doing?" You walk right up to your stressor. You face your enemy; you resist the devil and he shall flee.

He has a kingdom that is a bureaucracy; he has a body of sin in the earth executing his master plan. The devil is a big bully, full of fear, rejected and unloved. He wants you to enjoy his nature and become one with his torment. But we should be one with the peace of God!

Have you ever gone from fear of your stressor to panic just like that? That happens because the thought of a phobic object is sufficient to induce anxiety.

What is your stressor? Perfume? Cabbage? Food? Mold? Your pastor?

The psychological industry has said that our choice of the phobic symbol is often determined by a chance exposure to the object. And it comes at a time when the anxiety over a threatened inner impulse first appeared. Then, when the phobic object becomes a conditioned stimuli, the phobic neurosis is beneath that in a learned response.

They have also said the very thought of a phobic object can induce anxiety and as the patient comes closer in reality to the phobic stimulus, the anxiety mounts to an intensity reaching panic.

THE PERSONALITY OF FEAR

Fear is not the fight or flight God created you with for normal life circumstances, but an aberration. At some point, either in your family tree or in your personal life, there is the work of an evil spirit that is able to program your thinking long-term.

Hebrews 4:12 says the Word of God comes to separate your soul from your spirit. Why? Because you have become one spiritually with something that is not from God. Not only have you become one spiritually, you have become one with it in your soul and that connects to the body.

Your body is a responder to who you are in your spiritual dimension and who you are in your thinking.

Remember the Word says, "As a man thinketh in his heart, so is he." Psalm 23:7 So if you have a fearful heart, it could progress to the point that you develop a personality of Fear. It is not just having the spirit of Fear that would set you up and program you through protein synthesis in your memes, or your long-term memory. But Fear could become so much a part of you that it becomes part of your personality.

Psychoanalysis does have an element of truth. It is an observation of evil spirits in mankind: the identification of evil spirits working through man's soul, programming his thinking. Do you know that parts of your personality are really not you? Do you take time to stop and let the Holy Spirit teach you? How often do we spiritually cram our mouths full of manna and do not even know what we have eaten?

When the Bible says your mind is renewed by the washing of the water of the Word, it means new memes, attitude adjustments and personality changes are created. When you have an attitude adjustment, you have a personality change.

Do you think it is possible for parts of your personality to not even be what God created? There are people with split personalities. There are people who have type A personalities. There are people with multiple personalities. There are people who have a wide range of breakdown in thought. The Bible says a double minded man is unstable in all his ways.

A double minded man *is* unstable in all his ways. James 1:8

A double minded man is a person who has one foot in each kingdom. That person has a spiritual split personality! Part of his mind is aligned with what God said is truth and the other part of his mind is aligned with what the devil said is truth. Now whose report are you going to believe?

> **Who hath believed our report? and to whom is the arm of the LORD revealed?** Isaiah 53:1

Oh, I know you are saying, "God, I read two chapters in the Bible today." But what is the devil saying to you today? "What did you say, Satan? Tell me. I am no good? Yes, that's true." "I should be afraid of what? I hadn't thought about that. But thank you for reminding me. I should avoid that today."

Are you spiritually growing up or are you spiritually regressing? The Bible talks about us growing up; from glory to glory you are being changed into His image, the Father's image.

> **But we all, with open face beholding as in a glass the glory of the Lord, are changed into the same image from glory to glory, *even* as by the Spirit of the Lord.** 2 Corinthians 3:18

Jesus said, "If you have seen me, you have seen the Father." God the Father is not the Creator; Jesus Christ is. It says so in John 1, Colossians 1, Hebrews 1 and Genesis 1. God created all things through Jesus Christ.

Jesus Christ is the Creator and He is God the Word in heaven.

Now do you want to be double minded? Being double minded is where some of your torment comes from. You are unstable. We just read James 1:8, a double minded man is unstable in all his ways.

In the Holy Spirit you are the righteousness of God by faith. You are to be single minded, and you are to have the mind of Christ. If there is no Fear in Christ, then why should there be Fear in you? If you have the mind of Christ, you should not be full of Fear.

You have to develop a new way of thinking. Why do you keep believing a lie, making it so difficult to get the truth into you? Isn't it amazing how many lies you have listened to? You have listened to Unbelief and Doubt, an antichrist spirit.

Timothy says, "God has not given us the spirit of Fear, but of power (which is the Holy Ghost), love (which is the Father), and a sound mind (which is the Word of God, who is Jesus)." Amen!

> **For God hath not given us the spirit of fear; but of power, and of love, and of a sound mind.** 2 Timothy 1:7

Paul says in Romans,

> **For if ye live after the flesh...** Romans 8:13

The flesh is not the physical body. It is Satan's nature in you. It is what Paul said in Romans 7: it is the sin that dwells within you.

The flesh is what Jesus said in Mark 7. It is that evil that lives within you. It is the old man. It is the body of sin and it is hanging out on your couch, sitting in your armchair, sleeping in your bed and having breakfast, dinner, and lunch with you.

What happens if you let it hang out with you? If you live after the flesh and follow the spirit of Fear, you shall die. You die physically and you die spiritually.

Whatever you are following and allowing to remain in your life will become your weak spot. It will become the rotten potato that spoils the whole bin. What is not good for you that you allow to remain as part of your life will infect you. Not only will it infect you, it is a spiritual parasite and it will suck the life right out of you.

Fear is the substance of things *not* hoped for, the evidence *not* yet seen. Fear and faith are equal in this dimension. They both demand to be fulfilled. Fear is also a form of faith. It is Satan's faith. It is faith in the devil. Real faith comes from God. Have faith in God.

> **For if ye live after the flesh, ye shall die: but if ye through the Spirit do mortify the deeds of the body, ye shall live.**
> Romans 8:13

That word "mortify" means to kill, destroy, put to death. Well, who needs to get put to death, you or the devil? The devil. Who needs to live, you or the devil? You. I hope you really believe that, because if you don't have the will to believe that, you will never defeat it.

Galatians will help you understand the manifestation of spiritual things through the body.

> **Now the works of the flesh are manifest, which are *these;* Adultery, fornication, uncleanness, lasciviousness,**
> Galatians 5:19

Do you commit adultery in the human body, or do you commit it invisibly? Both. Because the Lord said, "He who looks at a woman and takes her in his heart and defiles her in his heart, has committed adultery with her already." Matthew 5:28

So did it begin in the actual act or in the spiritual dimension of his existence? Outside or inside?

Adultery does not begin with the act. The act is the fruit of the spiritual problem, which is the carnal nature of Satan. A person who commits adultery has an evil spirit of adultery.

Incubus and Succubus are evil spirits. One is the evil spirit that comes and has sex with a woman and the other comes and has sex with a man. People are awakened in the middle of the night, paralyzed by some invisible being that is having sexual relations with them. It is so well known that you can find it in *Webster's Dictionary*. It is a common occurrence.

You need to get free by dealing with anything in you linking up with it. There is a victimization spirit within you.

Fornication is the same thing as adultery; but fornication is between two people who are not married. Adultery is a sexual relationship between people who are married to someone else.

In a book about Carl Jung, there is a whole chapter on polygamy, orgies and multiple sexual partners as the ultimate form of psychotherapy. In other words, those who come out of Freudian and Jungian backgrounds teach the worst thing that can happen to you is to be civilized and to be married to one partner.

They teach monogamy is bondage and freedom is being animalistic—taking sex wherever you can find it. That is sick. That is actually what *produces* disease.

Is Hatred part of your body, part of your physical flesh? The Bible says the works of the flesh are manifest: uncleanness, lasciviousness, idolatry, witchcraft, hatred. So how do you manifest Hatred? It is an expression of your mind and your thinking.

Hatred is made manifest in the physical because of what you would say or do. Does it begin on the inside, or does it begin with the outside action? Jesus said back in Mark 7 the evil was in a person's heart.

You are going to have to put aside some very bad teaching that you are a sick personality already and that it is just your flesh. Even if it were just your flesh, you are still responsible for it and you are required to mortify and kill it.

Are you going to kill your human body? Is that what it means? Does it mean you put to death your arm, or your leg, or your nose, or your eye? No. It means to put to death the thing in you that is evil. That is what deliverance is all about.

How about Strife? Is strife a part of your physical body? Does it manifest? How about heresies? Are heresies part of your physical body? It says the works of the flesh are manifest.

Have you ever seen heresy on people? Have you ever seen heresy in the physical body? Where is it coming from? Out of their thinking. Where does it come from in their thinking?

There is a spirit of Divination at work that has taught them error and they are now preaching it. That is what heresy is. Where did that come from? It came out of the dimension of the spirit world into the spirit, into the five physical senses, into the soul. It became a thought and the thought was expressed.

The expression of heresy comes through writing with a pen or speaking with the mouth. It has authority inside the spirit and the soul of that being.

Let's go back over to Romans. "But if you through the spirit do mortify the deeds of the body, you shall live."

> **For if ye live after the flesh, ye shall die: but if ye through the Spirit do mortify the deeds of the body, ye shall live.**
> Romans 8:13

The deeds of the body are the works of the flesh. If you have Christ in you, how do you mortify the deeds of the body? Your body has a mind. Your body is expressing your thoughts when it stirs up strife in words. "That is my body saying that." When you punch someone's lights out, that is a deed of the flesh.

What made your body do it? Your body does not have a mind of its own. Your body has no brain cells. It has no spirit and it has no soul. It is just the house you live in and it is dangling on the end of a lot of neurological, biological and chemical realities to which it responds. But the origin of everything is inside.

> **For as many as are led by the Spirit of God, they are the sons of God.** Romans 8:14

"God has not given you the spirit of Fear, but of power, love and a sound mind." 2 Timothy 1:7 For as many as are led by the Spirit of God, they are the sons of God.

> **For ye have not received the spirit of bondage again to fear; but ye have received the Spirit of adoption, whereby we cry, Abba, Father.** Romans 8:15

For you have not received a spirit of Bondage again to Fear. Could I say it this way? To fear again is to be in Bondage again. God has not given you the spirit of Fear according to Timothy and Paul says you have not received a spirit of Bondage again to Fear. Fear is a spirit of Bondage!

Fear causes you to avoid people and your family. It will make you go hide somewhere. Is that freedom or is that Bondage? Fear is not a blessing. Fear is a curse and it produces bondage.

Did someone make you dress up the way you are today? Did someone come in and say, "You are going to wear this today," or did you just wear what you wanted?

Did someone come in and say, "You are going to wear this, this and this. You have to." Would that be freedom or Bondage? So why do you allow this thing to dress you up every day in Fear?

"Well," you say, "I am not going to wear you today."

"But you must wear Fear of man today! You are going to be afraid of everyone with whom you come in contact. You cannot look them in the eye and you are going to cross the street and not look up. You have Fear of man. Your mother does not like you; your mother hates you and you have Fear."

You say, "I must avoid people today." Besides that, the evil spirit comes to you and says, "Remember…? Remember…? Remember what they did to you?"

How about Fear of disease? It says, "I think you need to be afraid of cancer today. I think you need to be preoccupied with cancer. There is a smell in the air. I think there is a pesticide in it. I think you need to be preoccupied with where pesticides might be."

All day you are in this mindset of Fear. You look at someone and think, "Did you have lice? What did you use to get rid of it? I smell it on you!"

"Did you spray your house for roaches?" All day long you are dressed up in the Fear of pesticides. Long-term memory can make you think you smell something that is not there. You mostly remember the smell by suggestion, but you could think you smell it because your five physical senses are entwined that closely together. You can be "had" that easily.

You have not received the spirit of Bondage again to Fear, but you have received the Spirit of adoption, whereby we cry, 'Abba, Father.' The Spirit itself bears witness with our spirit that we are the children of God. When you have evil spirits, they bear witness with you that you are the children of the devil.

"Wait a minute. I am born again. You can't say that about me!"

Whatever you yield your members to, it becomes your master and you become its slave.

> **18Being then made free from sin, ye became the servants of righteousness.**
>
> **19I speak after the manner of men because of the infirmity of your flesh: for as ye have yielded your members servants to uncleanness and to iniquity unto iniquity; even so now yield your members servants to righteousness unto holiness.** Romans 6:18-19

Why do you call yourselves sons of God, but you yield your members to be slaves of the devil? Why do you call yourself children of God, yet you lend your members to the spirits of wickedness? It says whosoever is born of God cannot sin.

> **Whosoever is born of God doth not commit sin; for his seed remaineth in him: and he cannot sin, because he is born of God.** 1 John 3:9

Are you prepared, really, to accept your place in the family of God? What is the worst thing that can happen to you? You can die and go to heaven. Do you believe that? If not, then you would be a spiritual failure.

Who is on the throne? It is not what I want; it's what God wants me to do. It is not my world. It is not my will being done in earth as it is in heaven. It is *His* will being done on earth as it is in heaven.

How is His will done in the earth? The Holy Spirit only works through people, the people of God. This planet is for you and me, as His children, and for His kingdom.

About eight months after I came back to God, after years of wandering, I was called out of a meeting of 1,500 people. They did not even know my name. God spoke to me through the gifts, and I will never forget what God said: "You belong to Me. You are Mine. I have called you to do a work in your generation. Be all that I called you to be and do not listen to lies."

Now what was that word to me? Not my word, but His. I responded to that immediately and it glowed like a fire on the inside of my spirit. I don't know what all that means in my lifetime, but I know His will is being performed through me. I do not even try to create it. I just show up every day and what happens, happens.

What you need to do is just show up every day in faith and not in fear. Fear will drive you. Fear is the foundation for Witchcraft and one of the open doors for it, because Fear always "needs to know."

Witchcraft always needs to know. Divination always needs to know. We call it "the knowing one."

Have you ever run into a person who just has to know everything about you? They are plucking you apart. When you have a person who has a need to know everything, you have Divination. The need to know is rooted in Fear of tomorrow. You do not need to know anything; just show up.

The Bible says, "Take no thought for tomorrow because the evil of today is sufficient for the day."

> **Take therefore no thought for the morrow: for the morrow shall take thought for the things of itself. Sufficient unto the day *is* the evil thereof.** Matthew 6:34

We are so busy remembering the things of the past and projecting them into the future, we forget to take care of the evil here today. We wonder why we are having a bad day!

Can I say that to you again? You are so busy living in the past and projecting it into the future that you forget to defeat evil today. That is Fear!

Are you spending all your time living in the past and projecting it into the future? That is what Fear does to you. You do not trust God. You have a need to know. All the pieces have to be in place.

Faith is walking as far as you know how to walk in the natural and the next step is into black oblivion. That is where you are going because you do not even know what is in the path of the next step. But you just keep walking. You might find yourself walking on water one day! Amen?

This is a tremendous spiritual principle. When Peter walked on the water, everyone put him down, saying, "That old sorry thing! He shouldn't have taken his eyes off Jesus!" At least he tried it. That is more than the rest of them did.

Take no thought for tomorrow. Be anxious for nothing! Have no anxiety! Do not fear tomorrow.

> **The Spirit itself beareth witness with our spirit, that we are the children of God:** Romans 8:16

Fear is called a spirit of Bondage. There are synonyms for fear. Fear is a feeling, an anxious thought, a dread. Dread is the projection of Fear, the projection of evil into the future. Dread is expecting something to go wrong. How many of us struggle with that? You just know it is not going to go right today. Dread is expecting something unpleasant, often unknown or uncertain.

Another aspect of fear is alarm. Fight or flight is the mind-body connection. That is the sudden, startling fear. "Be not afraid of sudden fear, neither of the desolation of the wicked when it cometh, for the LORD shall be thy confidence and shall keep thy foot from being taken." Prov.erbs 3:25

"Be not afraid of sudden fear." What does that mean? Are you able to have a complete flaring of the mind-body connection? Are you going to be totally in fight or flight realities with your heart racing and your five physical senses on the alert—or are you able to stand there and not be in Fear? Can you face your enemy even though your thoughts are terrifying and your body is physically pitching a fit?

Sometimes things just happen. Do you know what Jesus said about the 18 men that died in that high-rise? Do you think these people were more evil than the people in the town that weren't killed?

> **4Or those eighteen, upon whom the tower in Siloam fell, and slew them, think ye that they were sinners above all men that dwelt in Jerusalem?**
>
> **5I tell you, Nay: but, except ye repent, ye shall all likewise perish.** Luke 13:4-5

Jesus said, "That is not the issue. The issue is this: Are you right with God? Because if you are right with God you shall live again." This life is just a season for you. Maybe you are a late blooming flower. We need you in your season!

Moses was a late blooming flower. He killed an Egyptian, then ran in fear from the Pharaoh and hid in the desert for 40 years. At age 80 he became a late blooming flower and for 40 years he busted hell wide open and let God's people go free!

Maybe in your season you can bust hell wide open! Get out of the mentality of mankind and get into the mentality of God who created you for His purposes and His plan and what He wants. He is able to keep that which you have committed to Him against that day, but if you do not believe it, it will never happen.

Be not afraid of alarm and sudden fear. Do not be afraid of Fear. That would be Fear of Fear. What overcomes Fear? Relationship with God. Perfect love. Trust. Faith.

The Scriptures say, "Faith comes by hearing and hearing by the Word of God." But you cannot have faith just by reading the Word. It is predicated on you trusting the Man who wrote it! Faith is directly related to trust. And when you trust, you have no Fear. If you have Fear, it means you do not trust God.

There is something within you that will not allow you to believe that God is able. You say, "But if God is able, then why do I have this problem?" That is the first thing that is recovered out of Unbelief and Doubt, Accusing spirits against God.

"Well, if God loves me and I'm trusting Him, why do I have this problem?"

You have the problem because of Deuteronomy 28, Leviticus 26, Deuteronomy 25 and Proverbs 26:2. The curse without a cause does not come.

> **As the bird by wandering, as the swallow by flying, so the curse causeless shall not come.** Proverbs 26:2

It did not come from God, because the Word says God does not tempt men with evil, neither can He be tempted with it.

> **Let no man say when he is tempted, I am tempted of God: for God cannot be tempted with evil, neither tempteth he any man:** James 1:13

So evil does not come from God!

Oh, I know what it says in the law that God created evil. Isaiah 45:7 The Hebrew meaning of that word "create" is also "cut down." But you have to understand this in the context of what the Jewish people thought about good and evil at that time. They did not understand the devil.

People do not want to serve God because they are double minded. They do not want to serve God. They do not want to be good; they want to be evil. It is a calculated decision.

They say, "Oh, it overcame me." No, it did not! You had been meditating on it for days! It's just that now it has manifested. It had been there all along. It did not overtake you suddenly.

"Oh, the devil made me do it." No, he did not. *You* did it. Paul said, "It is the sin within me." Oh, yes, sin did it *through* you, but you agreed, didn't you? Then it becomes your sin.

When you become one with sin, you become a sinner in that area of your life. You need to repent. Sin does not get a chance to repent, but you do.

NOT TRUSTING GOD

Job said,

> **Though he slay me, yet will I trust in him...** Job 13:15

What do you trust Him for? It does not make any difference if you live or you die. Trust is – you believe God has things in control.

Receiving things from God is not even the object of trust. It is a state of being. You do not have to receive anything from God to trust Him. You believe God just because He is. You love God just because He is, not because of what He does for you.

You have to believe the scripture that says when you are in covenant with God, you shall never die. You have to believe there is life after death. You have to believe you are complete in Him.

Trust is absolute confidence. Trust in God is confidence in Him whether you are healed or not. You always have faith for healing, of course, but that has nothing to do with trust.

What is the worst thing that can happen to you? You are not healed. You are going to die and go to heaven anyway. It is appointed unto man once to die and then the judgment. So whether we die at age 39 or 99, at some point within a hundred years, we are going to die. Then there's the resurrection. That is the completeness of understanding.

We do not *want* to die at 39, because Moses prophesied in Psalm 90 that the longevity of man shall be 70 to 80 years. That is the blessing. A shortened life is a curse and that comes from sin, either from a family sin or personal sin. It can also come from tragedy.

But when accidents happen and people lose their lives, don't accuse God. Jesus dealt with that when He talked about the men who were killed by the tower that fell.

The point is this: Are you right with God?

Accidents happen, but in the day of resurrection you shall live again. You have to settle this! If you don't, you will have Fear of Death and Fear of dying. So what happens if you think your entire existence is wrapped up in this little life you have? This little life you have is a drop in the bucket compared to eternity.

Now, I trust God whether I live or I die. It does not make any difference. If I have a problem in life, I ask God for freedom. He tells me to ask. Does He ask me to apply my heart to righteousness? Yes. I am the product of that and I am working out my own salvation daily with fear and trembling, according to the Scriptures. Philippians 2:12

If mankind had not fallen, if mankind had never sinned, we would not have to worry about disease, because there would be none. Disease is the product of sin. That is what it says in Deuteronomy 28, concerning blessings and cursings. This entire chapter lays out the benefits of obedience and the results of disobedience.

Also, Deuteronomy says,

> **And the LORD will take away from thee all sickness, and will put none of the evil diseases of Egypt...** Deuteronomy 7:15

That is also what it says in Proverbs,

> **...so the curse causeless shall not come.** Proverbs 26:2

So if we are diseased, it is because we and our ancestors have sinned against God. Disease is the result of our not loving God and not obeying God at some point in our ancestral line or in our personal lives. It doesn't have anything to do with trusting God. This is our problem, not God's problem. Faith is the substance of things hoped for.

Mark says,

> **And Jesus answering saith unto them, Have faith in God.**
> Mark 11:22

What does that mean? It means to trust Him in all things—in your sin and not just in your salvation. That is what grace and mercy is all about.

JOURNEY TO HEALING

We have many promises of provision from God.

> **...yet ye have not, because ye ask not.** James 4:2

> **Is any sick among you? let him call for the elders of the church; and let them pray over him, anointing him with oil in the name of the Lord:** James 5:14

> **Beloved, I wish above all things that thou mayest prosper and be in health, even as thy soul prospereth.** 3 John 1:2

Thessalonians gives a spiritual, psychological and biological provision for health.

> **And the very God of peace sanctify you wholly; and *I pray God* your whole spirit and soul and body be preserved blameless unto the coming of our Lord Jesus Christ.**
> 1 Thessalonians 5:23

Between our current state and receiving the promise we are coming out of bondage. So we still need to trust God as we are being changed. I trust God whether I live or whether I die.

If I were to die today—God forbid, because I want to damage that other kingdom for a few more years—but if I did, I would still be complete. My faith is that God has called me to do something in my generation and I am not going to lay my spirit down to any devil until I have finished the call of God in my life.

If I have a sin that would shorten my life, I ask God to reveal it so I can get it dealt with and live longer. Do you understand where I am coming from? I am as susceptible to the curse as you are.

There may be things in my life that will shorten it. I have the call of God on my life, so I tell God, "Show them to me. Do not let the devil rip me off. Bring it to my attention. I need my life."

In my thinking, I am not afraid of death or disease. Do you know where I go in my thinking sometimes—especially if someone says, "Well, you are getting old, Pastor"? Do you know where I go in faith? Even if I cannot stand behind the pulpit, you cannot shut my mouth. As long as I have breath, I can talk, I can write and I can speak on some dimension.

I am a warrior and I will go on fighting right to the end. That is my faith. I am going to live and not die and fulfill the call of God in my generation. That is my personal declaration.

I am going to fulfill the call of God on my life

The devil comes and says, "Okay, big guy, watch this," and he starts to project all the reasons why I will die. Does he try to stagger my belief in God? Absolutely.

Do you think I am going to listen to it? Do you think it is possible to have faith in the midst of extreme Fear? Do you think it is possible to believe God when Unbelief and Doubt are screaming in your ears? Do you think it is possible to believe in life when Death is knocking at your door?

So who are we listening to? Why are we listening to our enemy? Guard your heart. Make a resolution in your heart to just lay down your life. Trusting God means you decrease so He may increase.

> **For whosoever will save his life shall lose it: and whosoever will lose his life for my sake shall find it.**
>
> Matthew 16:25

Why does it say that he who tries to save his life shall lose it? Because that person has become a god to himself in Fear and he does not trust God.

But if you lose your life you shall gain it, because then you allow God to take over your life and perfect Himself in you. Fear demands to be fulfilled and God knows this.

Job said, "The thing that I feared the most has come upon me." Everything you fear needs to be crucified, put to death, mortified and be dealt with. Because Fear demands to be fulfilled. It has nothing to do with trusting God. It has nothing to do with God's provision. According to your faith, so be it unto you.

Fear is a form of faith

According to your faith, so be it unto you. If Fear is a form of faith and you believe what Fear says and not what God says, then according to your Fear-faith so be it unto you. Both are demanding to be fulfilled.

Receiving from God

Ishmael and Hagar

There is a very powerful principle in Genesis 21. This is where Hagar and Ishmael are sent away by Abraham. Hagar took the child, departed and wandered in the wilderness of Beersheba. When the water was spent in the bottle, she cast the child under one of the shrubs.

> **14And Abraham rose up early in the morning, and took bread, and a bottle of water, and gave *it* unto Hagar, putting *it* on her shoulder, and the child, and sent her away: and she departed, and wandered in the wilderness of Beer-sheba.**
>
> **15And the water was spent in the bottle, and she cast the child under one of the shrubs.**
>
> **16And she went, and sat her down over against *him* a good way off, as it were a bowshot: for she said, Let me not see the death of the child. And she sat over against *him*, and lift up her voice, and wept.** Genesis 21:14-16

Was she concerned about herself first or the child? She did not want to see the child die of thirst in the wilderness. Do you think Death was at the door?

> **And God heard the voice of the lad...** Genesis 21:17

The lad was crying too. Hagar was facing Fear of Death.

> **...and the angel of God called Hagar out of heaven, and said unto her, What aileth thee, Hagar?** Genesis 21:17

What are the next two words? "FEAR NOT."

> **17...fear not; for God hath heard the voice of the lad where he is.**

> **[18]Arise, lift up the lad, and hold him in thine hand; for I will make him a great nation.** Genesis 21:17-18

The Arabs are that great nation in verse 18 that will be saved in the millennium. In Isaiah, it says the sons of Kedar, the great-grandson of Ishmael, shall be gathered to Jerusalem to the King. Isaiah 60 The Arabs are the first people to be saved and restored in the natural nations of the earth in the millennium.

The Arabs shall accept Jesus as the Messiah. Then they shall be reunited with their half brothers the Jews and be one forever. Hallelujah! That is the promise, right in the book of Isaiah. That is a good peace pact, isn't it? The Prince of Peace is able to broker that one.

You should start praying for the Arabs. Do not curse them. They are just in Rejection. They have a massive spirit of Rejection which they inherited from generation to generation. Ask that their eyes be opened and that they be delivered from Islam. Pray, because they are a blessed people of God. They just have not seen the fulfillment of the blessing yet, but it is coming.

> **[19]And God opened her eyes, and she saw a well of water; and she went, and filled the bottle with water, and gave the lad drink.**
>
> **[20]And God was with the lad; and he grew, and dwelt in the wilderness, and became an archer.**
>
> **[21]And he dwelt in the wilderness of Paran: and his mother took him a wife out of the land of Egypt.** Genesis 21:19-21

So this is the story of Ishmael and Hagar. Hagar was afraid of Death. God told her to fear not because He had heard the cries of the child.

What was the fulcrum point of receiving?

Number one, believing God.

Number two, not fearing.

What happened next? In the midst of that, God opened her eyes so she could see.

Fear is a form of blindness. Fear can paralyze you neurologically.

Have you ever seen anyone paralyzed by Fear? Have you ever shut down mentally because of Fear? Has your ability to think properly shut down because of panic?

Fear is a form of blindness that clouds out the faith to defeat it. Is it possible to be blind and yet still see? Yes. Fear is also a form of eyesight. In phobias and panic attacks you are seeing with the eyes of Fear.

Do you think it is possible for you to see with the eyes of Hatred? Have you ever considered this? When you become obsessed with something, isn't that tunnel vision? Isn't that a form of eyesight?

You can become so obsessed with something it consumes all your thoughts. That is a form of eyesight.

What does the Spirit of God use to give you eyesight? The Word. The Word of God is that lamp that allows you to see.

> **Thy word *is* a lamp unto my feet, and a light unto my path.** Psalm 119:105

> **The spirit of man *is* the candle of the LORD, searching all the inward parts of the belly.** Proverbs 20:27

The Word of God in your human spirit is the light, and that is the candle of the living Word. You are either the candle of the LORD or you are a black light. Would you rather be a white light or a black light?

Black light is depressing. It is dark. It is still light, but it is a dark light. One of the parables talks about your little candle and not hiding it under a bushel.

> **15Neither do men light a candle, and put it under a bushel, but on a candlestick; and it giveth light unto all that are in the house.**
>
> **16Let your light so shine before men, that they may see your good works, and glorify your Father which is in heaven.** Matthew 5:15-16

What do you do with your candle? You let it shine, let it shine, let it shine. "Let your light so shine before men that they may see your good works and glorify your Father." You say you have faith. Show your faith by your works. "Faith without works is dead."

> **17Even so faith, if it hath not works, is dead, being alone.**
>
> **18Yea, a man may say, Thou hast faith, and I have works: shew me thy faith without thy works, and I will shew thee my faith by my works.**
>
> **19Thou believest that there is one God; thou doest well: the devils also believe, and tremble.**
>
> **20But wilt thou know, O vain man, that faith without works is dead?** James 2:17-20

FEAR COMING OUT OF A CURSE

The death of Rachel is recorded in Genesis.

> **16And they journeyed from Bethel; and there was but a little way to come to Ephrath: and Rachel travailed, and she had hard labour.**
>
> **17And it came to pass, when she was in hard labour, that the midwife said unto her, Fear not; thou shalt have this son also.** Genesis 35:16-17

Rachel had Fear of losing the child in childbirth. Rachel died in childbirth. Do you know why? Her husband cursed her with death for stealing from her father and lying about the idol when he did not know she had lied. She took with her an object of idolatry from pagan worship.

When Laban came to look for his favorite idol he worshipped, he said, "Someone has stolen it."

Jacob said, "Whosoever has stolen your idol, let them be cursed with death. They shall die for it." They came into the tent where Rachel had hidden the idol. She was sitting on it on a camel's pad or saddle, pretending she was having her monthly cycle.

Rachel said, "Oh, I can't get up. I have PMS today." She lied to her husband and she lied to her father. She had taken the object of idolatry herself.

Your words have power. If you have ever cursed anyone to hell or death, you need to repent because those words are demanding to be fulfilled. The same curse with which you curse another will come back into your own bowels. You need to bless and not curse.

If you have cursed others, get before God *today, now,* and remember their faces and repent. Pull those words down. Separate the sin from the people and release them to either salvation or judgment. It is not our duty either to save or to judge. It is our business to release.

Get it right with every person who has ever wronged you and release them

When you forgive others, you do not have to condone what they did. You can still hate the evil, but you cannot hate the people who hurt you, because Jesus died for them. The Bible says you are to have a perfect hatred for evil.

[21]Do not I hate them, O Lord, that hate thee? and am not I grieved with those that rise up against thee?

[22]I hate them with perfect hatred: I count them mine enemies. Psalm 139:21-22

Some people say, "Well, I can't forgive them because in forgiving them I will let them off the hook and condone what they did." Boy, did you buy a lie! You are not condoning anything. You are not letting anyone off the hook. You are getting it done the way God wants you to get it done. Release them! But never condone the evil.

Are you able not to condone the evil in a person, but love the person? God did that for the whole world when He came into a very evil world that cursed Him and hated Him. He stood in the name of love to save us. You and I have responded to that, praise God! If you think love is based on someone else loving you, you can forget it.

Love is your nature regardless of whether it is received or not

So Rachel had Fear of losing the child in childbirth and the midwife said to her, "Fear not, you shall have this son also." What a powerful statement of faith!

Paul explains in Hebrews why we no longer have to fear Death.

[14]Forasmuch then as the children are partakers of flesh and blood, he also himself likewise took part of the same; that through death he might destroy him that had the power of death, that is, the devil;

[15]And deliver them who through fear of death were all their lifetime subject to bondage. Hebrews 2:14-15

Because Jesus became a man like you and me and He went to His death, we do not have to fear Death anymore.

Did Jesus have Fear of Death? Only for a moment, but He subjected that Fear to the will of God. He said, "Father, if it be possible, take this cup from me, but nevertheless, not my will, but thine be done." Luke 22:42

That is trust! Could it be that Job prophesied about Jesus, "Though God slay me, yet will I trust him"?

> **Though he slay me, yet will I trust in him: but I will maintain mine own ways before him.** Job 13:15

The Bible says God the Father turned His face from Jesus when He died and let Him die. Then Jesus could have said, "Though God slay me, yet will I trust Him." You and I are eternally saved because of that action. You and I would be dead in our sins today if Jesus had gone into Fear. Trusting God is the antidote for Fear.

"God has not given you the spirit of Fear, but power, love and a sound mind." 2 Timothy 1:7 This verse contains the Holy Spirit (power), the Father (love) and Jesus the Word (sound mind).

Fellowship with the Godhead will always replace Satan in relationship.

"And deliver them who through Fear of Death were all their lifetime subject to bondage." Hebrews 2:15 What is the number one fear in mankind today as human beings? Fear of dying. Fear of Death. Paul calls Fear of dying bondage.

The Bible also says, "You have not received the spirit of Bondage again to fear, but the Spirit of adoption whereby we can cry out, Abba, Father." Romans 8:15 What is the worst thing that can happen to you? You can die and go to heaven to be with the Father.

JACOB'S FEARS

Let's look at Fear of tomorrow in Genesis.

> **[1]And Israel took his journey with all that he had, and came to Beer-sheba, and offered sacrifices unto the God of his father Isaac.**
>
> **[2]And God spake unto Israel in the visions of the night, and said, Jacob, Jacob. And he said, Here *am* I.**
>
> **[3]And he said, I *am* God, the God of thy father: fear not to go down into Egypt; for I will there make of thee a great nation:**
>
> **[4]I will go down with thee into Egypt; and I will also surely bring thee up *again:* and Joseph shall put his hand upon thine eyes.** Genesis 46:1-4

This is Jacob going into Egypt. What did God say to Israel (Jacob)? Fear not to go down into Egypt. This is Fear of the future or Fear of tomorrow.

Joseph's brothers also had Fear of tomorrow. They fell down before his face. "Behold we be thy servants, and Joseph said unto them, 'fear not... for you thought evil against me, but God meant it unto good.' "

> **[18]And his brethren also went and fell down before his face; and they said, Behold, we *be* thy servants.**
>
> **[19]And Joseph said unto them, Fear not: for *am* I in the place of God?**
>
> **[20]But as for you, ye thought evil against me; *but* God meant it unto good, to bring to pass, as *it is* this day, to save much people alive.**
>
> **[21]Now therefore fear ye not: I will nourish you, and your little ones. And he comforted them, and spake kindly unto them.** Genesis 50:18-21

What the devil planned for our evil, God will turn for good. Genesis 50:20 is the foundation for that spiritual thought. What the devil plans against you for destruction, God will turn it for good.

Joseph said to his brothers, "As for you, you thought evil against me, but God meant it for good, to bring it to pass as it is this day to save much people alive. Now therefore fear ye not."

Joseph's brothers were afraid of the future.

They also had Fear of man, Fear of judgment, Fear of being killed. They had lots of Fear. Joseph must have seen it and told them not to be afraid. "Fear not, I will nourish you and your little ones. Be comforted. " And he comforted and spake kindly unto them.

What a guy! What would you do if your brothers and sisters had taken you and sold you into slavery and ripped you off and threatened to kill you? Would you nourish them? Would you nurture them—or make them pay?

In Exodus, when the Israelites were being led out of Egypt by Moses, we find another kind of fear. This is right before God parted the waters in the Red Sea.

> **10 And when Pharaoh drew nigh, the children of Israel lifted up their eyes, and, behold, the Egyptians marched after them; and they were sore afraid: and the children of Israel cried out unto the LORD.**
>
> **11 And they said unto Moses, Because *there were* no graves in Egypt, hast thou taken us away to die in the wilderness? wherefore hast thou dealt thus with us, to carry us forth out of Egypt?**
>
> **12 *Is* not this the word that we did tell thee in Egypt, saying, Let us alone, that we may serve the Egyptians? For *it had been* better for us to serve the Egyptians, than that we should die in the wilderness.** Exodus 14:10-12

Do you know what Fear will do to you? Fear will take you right back into Bondage and you will say, "I want to stay sick. I want to be paranoid. I want to have anxiety."

"Pastor, how dare you go in there and stir this mess up! I was content in my bondage."

Do you know how many people do not want to be delivered and do not want to be free? When you face your fears you are going to have to be prepared to go all the way, even if your enemy is munching at your tail.

Fear demands that you fold and go back down under. The Israelites said, "Now, Moses, we do not want to be delivered. Leave us alone. You brought us here to die."

This is the enemy right here. They were afraid of danger. They were afraid of a problem. "For it would have been better for us to serve the Egyptians than that we should die in the wilderness."

> **And Moses said unto the people, Fear ye not, stand still, and see the salvation of the LORD, which he will shew to you to day: for the Egyptians whom ye have seen to day, ye shall see them again no more for ever.** Exodus 14:13

"And Moses said unto the people, Fear not. Stand still." What do you do with Fear? When having done all, stand.

> **Wherefore take unto you the whole armour of God, that ye may be able to withstand in the evil day, and having done all, to stand.** Ephesians 6:13

Taking a Stand

What do you do with Fear? You stand still!

> **Be still, and know that I *am* God: I will be exalted among the heathen, I will be exalted in the earth.** Psalm 46:10

When you turn your back to run, you have had it!

What have you been told to do? Fear not. Stand. What does Fear want to make you do? In biology the first part of a fear syndrome is called fight or flight.

Why is it called fight or flight? Because when you are up against your stressor and your fear object, you are going to do one of two things. You are either going to stand and fight or run and take flight. What are you going to do?

Are you going to fight? Or are you going to flee? If you flee, you are being programmed to flee and take flight every time. If you fight, God is with you. If you flee, Satan is with you.

The word "Jehovah" literally means "mighty in battle." The idea is that when you stand against your enemy, you are not alone. Jehovah the Lord is with you. But in this dispensation of time, who has He sent to empower you over your enemy? The Holy Spirit; He is also God. You are not alone because the Holy Spirit lives in you.

Do you have the Holy Spirit in you? He is there and Fear is there. Your stressor is there. It is fight or flight. In the day that you turn in flight, the Holy Spirit is grieved and He does not do anything for you at all.

But, when you get back in Bondage, He comes slowly and gently and starts to work with you again to bring you not to freedom, but back in the face of the enemy. You cannot be free if you do not face your enemy!

Read the Old Testament. No freedom ever came unless the children of Israel faced the enemy and they faced the enemy many times in fear.

Now when you face the enemy, you are not only facing him in faith, you are facing him in fear. Everything that Fear represents is thundering through you. So you are not only facing the enemy in faith, you are facing the enemy in fear. Then you stand and let the Lord fight your battle!

> **...When the enemy shall come in like a flood, the Spirit of the LORD shall lift up a standard against him.** Isaiah 59:19

Here is the problem. You are a physical being. You are standing against an invisible enemy that is terrorizing you and you have to believe in an invisible Helper. It is so amazing that you will listen to the invisible enemy more than you will listen to the invisible Helper! That is part of your Fear!

Fear is designed to steal your faith. If Satan cannot keep you from being born again, through Fear he will keep you from being effective against him as a Christian. Jesus said many times, "Fear not, I am with you."

Do you remember when Elisha was in tribulation about some stuff and the heavens opened up? He saw a whole army on the mountain and the Lord said, "There are more fer ya than there are agin' ya."

He did not really say it just that way, but that's what it means: "There are more for you than there are against you."

> **16And he answered, Fear not: for they that *be* with us *are* more than they that *be* with them.**

[17]**And Elisha prayed, and said, LORD, I pray thee, open his eyes, that he may see. And the LORD opened the eyes of the young man; and he saw: and, behold, the mountain *was* full of horses and chariots of fire round about Elisha.**

2 Kings 6:16-17

If you only knew the powers of God's angelic forces that are at your disposal when you are standing!

Now Daniel prayed and it was 21 days before the answer came. For 21 days there was warfare in heaven to keep that answer from coming through.

[2]**In those days I Daniel was mourning three full weeks.**

[13]**But the prince of the kingdom of Persia withstood me one and twenty days: but, lo, Michael, one of the chief princes, came to help me; and I remained there with the kings of Persia.** Daniel 10:2, 13

Fear will not let you stand for 21 days. If it does not happen instantly when you are believing, you fold. On the day that you fold, you are programmed to fold from then on.

I made up my mind I am going to believe and trust God whether He does one thing for me or not. My belief and trust in God has nothing to do with receiving. It has to do with believing.

What were the children of Israel doing? They were in fight or flight. They wanted to flee or take flight.

Moses told them, "Fear not, God is here." God opened the waters and they walked through on dry ground. As the enemy came onto the dry ground behind them, the waters closed and the enemy and their chariots were destroyed and consumed by the waters.

That is the beauty of defeating Fear. Your enemy is destroyed right behind you. When you are standing against your enemy, he is defeated. Well, you're not just standing;

you're standing according to knowledge. Many people are standing believing God for healing, but they have not worked out the Roots and the Blocks. So it is not just as simple as believing.

Many churches teach you how to believe, but only five percent of anyone ever receives. Why do 95 percent fail? Because of what it says in Isaiah and Hosea. God said, "My people have gone into captivity because they have no knowledge."

"My people perish for lack of knowledge." It is not that God cannot or will not heal. It is not that you cannot stand. It is that we are ignorant and have lost our way.

> **Therefore my people are gone into captivity, because *they have* no knowledge: and their honourable men *are* famished, and their multitude dried up with thirst.** Isaiah 5:13

> **My people are destroyed for lack of knowledge: because thou hast rejected knowledge, I will also reject thee, that thou shalt be no priest to me: seeing thou hast forgotten the law of thy God, I will also forget thy children.** Hosea 4:6

But you have the Word and "Faith comes by hearing and hearing by the Word of God." Romans 10:17

You have the Word to give you the faith to look at your roots and to stand against your enemy. If you find any of these things in your life that would keep you from being free of Fear and if you cohabit with any of this stuff and let it be part of your life, then you will be in flight instead of fight every time you turn around.

The people who are being healed of fear-anxiety disorders have learned these principles. God has met them in every single battle. It does not mean they win every time, because they were programmed to Fear over a period of time.

Your mind is renewed by the washing of the water of the Word. It is not an instant deluge; it is a process of time. Line upon line, line upon line, precept upon precept, precept upon precept. Here a little, there a little and gradually you walk out of this mess!

> **And be renewed in the spirit of your mind;** Ephesians 4:23

> **That he might sanctify and cleanse it with the washing of water by the word,** Ephesians 5:26

When you are facing your Fear, you stand. When you are going against your enemy, remember that three steps forward and two steps backward is still forward progress. But when you take three forward and two backward, Fear comes and says, "God's not with you." Well, what about that one-step victory you just won?

Fear makes you forget the victory and focuses on the things that are still not done—to cancel what He *did* do. As you are standing, all of a sudden you are one, two, three forward and only one back. Now you are two ahead today. Maybe the next day it is three forward and you lose no ground. That is how you walk out of Satan's kingdom, step-by-step.

Faith and Drivenness

Faith leads. Fear drives. "For as many as are led by the Spirit of God are the sons of God." Romans 8:14 "The LORD is my shepherd. I shall not want. He leadeth me beside the still waters." Psalm 23:1-2

Fear does not lead you; it drives you. Drivenness is an aspect of Fear. If you feel driven to do anything, you had better put the brakes on. Take time out. Go get some coffee. Take a nap. Do something else.

Faith represents the Good Shepherd. Fear represents the evil taskmaster. Faith represents freedom. Fear represents Bondage. "You have not been given the spirit of bondage again to fear." Romans 8:15

Faith is freedom. Fear is Bondage. Fear drives you. Faith leads you. "Faith comes by hearing and hearing by the Word of God." Romans 10:17 You follow the Word, the Light. Fear is darkness and Bondage.

Let's read.

> **7And it came to pass, when the children of Israel cried unto the LORD because of the Midianites,**
>
> **8That the LORD sent a prophet unto the children of Israel, which said unto them, Thus saith the LORD God of Israel, I brought you up from Egypt, and brought you forth out of the house of bondage;**
>
> **9And I delivered you out of the hand of the Egyptians, and out of the hand of all that oppressed you, and drave them out from before you, and gave you their land;**
>
> **10And I said unto you, I *am* the LORD your God; fear not the gods of the Amorites, in whose land ye dwell: but ye have not obeyed my voice.** Judges 6:7-10

Do not have Fear of the god of the Amorites—Fear of idol gods. Many people are afraid of evil religions and of the word "satanism" because they are afraid that Satan is all powerful. The word "voodoo" also generates Fear.

Some traditional religious practitioners are involved in necromancy. They sacrifice chickens, rabbits, cats and other animals to the deities, their ancestors. It's happening right in Miami and New York City, but "Be not afraid of their gods."

Let's read again.

> **35With whom the LORD had made a covenant, and charged them saying, Ye shall not fear other gods, nor bow yourselves to them, nor serve them, nor sacrifice to them:**
>
> **36But the LORD, who brought you up out of the land of Egypt with great power and a stretched out arm, him shall ye fear, and him shall ye worship, and to him shall ye do sacrifice.**
>
> **37And the statutes, and the ordinances, and the law, and the commandment, which he wrote for you, ye shall observe to do for evermore; and ye shall not fear other gods.**
>
> **38And the covenant that I have made with you ye shall not forget; neither shall ye fear other gods.** 2 Kings 17:35-38

Job says,

> **13In thoughts from the visions of the night, when deep sleep falleth on men,**
>
> **14Fear came upon me, and trembling, which made all my bones to shake.** Job 4:13-14

What came in the vision in the dream? "Fear came upon me and trembling, which made all my bones to shake." There is Fear from night torment.

The book of Psalms says,

> **5Thou shalt not be afraid for the terror by night; *nor* for the arrow *that* flieth by day;**

> [6]***Nor* for the pestilence *that* walketh in darkness; *nor* for the destruction *that* wasteth at noonday.** Psalm 91:5-6

"The terror by night." "The pestilence that walketh in darkness." Night terror is a big one, dreams and visions with respect to Fear. There is also Fear of the dark.

God wants you to know that He understands what you go through. He gave you scriptures to help you.

> **Yea, though I walk through the valley of the shadow of death, I will fear no evil: for thou *art* with me; thy rod and thy staff they comfort me.** Psalm 23:4

Fear of Death could be Fear of terrible diseases that produce death, or it could be Fear of anything that might cause death like Fear of accidents or Fear of being murdered. Fear of evil is common.

Do you "Fear no evil" only when you are not around it, or do you "Fear no evil" when you are right in the midst of it? Fear of evil could be one of two things. It could be projected or it could be real. "I will fear no evil." Why? "For Thou art with me, thy rod and thy staff, they comfort me."

> **Thou preparest a table before me in the presence of mine enemies: thou anointest my head with oil; my cup runneth over.** Psalm 23:5

"Thou preparest a table before me in the very presence of mine enemies." Fear of man and Fear of enemies. How about Fear of the IRS? How about Fear of the government?

Who would be your enemy? A mother-in-law that hates you. A bully. An enemy could be someone who wants to victimize you, someone who stalks you.

Your enemy could be someone who lies about you, slanders you and puts you down. David talked about his enemies being men that slandered him, wanted to kill him and meant evil toward him. This included friends who later became his enemies.

It says in Proverbs,

> [21]**My son, let not them depart from thine eyes: keep sound wisdom and discretion:**
>
> [22]**So shall they be life unto thy soul, and grace to thy neck.**
>
> [23]**Then shalt thou walk in thy way safely, and thy foot shall not stumble.**
>
> [24]**When thou liest down, thou shalt not be afraid: yea, thou shalt lie down, and thy sleep shall be sweet.** Proverbs 3:21-24

"Them" refers to wisdom and understanding. We get wisdom and understanding from the Word of God. "Let them not depart from thine eyes" so you can see where you are going. You need to keep sound wisdom and discretion.

"When you lie down, you shall not be afraid." That means sleeping at night without Fear. One of the greatest blessings of being a child of God is peaceable sleep at night, without torment and Fear.

"Yea, you shall lie down and thy sleep shall be sweet." Sweet sleep is a blessing.

Leviticus says,

> [6]**And I will give peace in the land, and ye shall lie down, and none shall make *you* afraid: and I will rid evil beasts out of the land, neither shall the sword go through your land.**
>
> [7]**And ye shall chase your enemies, and they shall fall before you by the sword.** Leviticus 26:6-7

What happens when you face your enemy? Resist the devil and he shall do what? Flee. James 4:7

The gates of hell shall not prevail or stand against the forward motion of the church. That means in the power of God by His Word, we march into enemy territory and take that turf back from him and establish the kingdom of God.

You need to consider your life your "land." You have a sovereign turf that belongs to you. Occupying your land and taking back your life is removing the beasts, the critters, the creatures and the parasites that interfere with your peace, your piece of life.

Ezekiel 34 is an indictment by the Father against the shepherds and pastors that are not taking care of God's people. They were not healing their diseases, they were not taking care of them and the people were scattered and became prey to all the beasts of the field.

Does it mean God's people were eaten by bears and lions and donkeys? The beast of the field is a spiritual metaphor dealing with satanic powers that oppress and put God's people in bondage because there is no one to shepherd them.

One of the messages of ministry is to raise up the church to start taking care of its people! The church is so busy preaching promise, it forgot to teach discernment. Promise without discernment is still Bondage. Discernment is a faculty of maturity.

"I will give you peace. You shall lie down and none shall make you afraid."

It says in Proverbs,

> **But whoso hearkeneth unto me shall dwell safely, and shall be quiet from fear of evil.** Proverbs 1:33

"But whoso hearkeneth to me..." The predication of freedom from Fear is hearkening unto God's Word—believing Him, believing what He said.

It says in the Psalms, "The Lord is my light and my salvation, whom shall I fear?"

> [1]**The Lord *is* my light and my salvation; whom shall I fear? the LORD *is* the strength of my life; of whom shall I be afraid?**
>
> [2]**When the wicked, *even* mine enemies and my foes, came upon me to eat up my flesh, they stumbled and fell.** Psalm 27:1-2

The LORD is the strength of my life. Of whom shall I be afraid? What is the antidote for Fear of man? Trusting the LORD!

"When the wicked, even mine enemies and my foes came upon me to eat up my flesh, they stumbled and fell." That takes care of Fear of man.

When you are in ministry, you are blessed by some people and cursed by others. I have not seen one person ever prosper that touched me and came against me. I have watched them stumble and fall and have seen tragedies come upon their lives.

The Word says,

> **...Touch not mine anointed, and do my prophets no harm.** Psalm 105:15

I would suggest very strongly that if you have a problem with your pastor, you get it right with him privately. Do not touch him. Do not gossip. Do not murmur. Do not complain.

Perfect love covers a multitude of sins. God's anointed and God's pastors and leaders are very special to Him. Just remember what happened to Miriam and Korah and Judas in their rebellion.

Fear Tied to the Unloving Spirit

Recent studies show that anxiety and stress are as detrimental to heart health as are cholesterol, smoking and others. You have to get rid of your anxieties and fears because they are detrimental to your health.

Fear, stress and anxiety probably account for at least 50 to 70 percent of all disease known to mankind. What people do not realize is that Fear, stress and anxiety many times are coupled with the Unloving spirit.

Fear is directly tied to not being loved and not feeling safe

To be free of Fear, you must be able to receive love and feel safe in it, regardless of whether anyone loves you or not. God loves you. An Unloving spirit and the spirit of Fear are antichrist spirits because they debate and dethrone the Word of God in your life.

When God says He loves you and you say you are not loved, you call God a liar. When God says, "Fear not," yet you continue to fear, you are calling God a liar again.

The phrases "Fear not" or "Do not fear" are found in the Bible more than 350 different times. Do you think God is trying to tell you something?

You must resolve the fact that you belong here on this planet and you must believe that God placed you here in your generation. You are going to have to believe the Word of God! You are not an accident! You were known from the foundation of the world.

"Before you were ever conceived genetically, all your parts and your pieces and who you are were known to Him." Psalm 139:15-16 Do you know what David said? "In sin my mother did conceive me." Psalm 51:5 Are you greater than David? He was a man after God's own heart. Acts 13:22

Yet you say you are not loved! You need to get a reality check. It is time you leave the past behind and get on with God from the foundation of the world. You are going to have to mix this with your faith and believe it, because it is in the Word.

One of the great turning points in my life personally in the area of an Unloving spirit and Fear was when I received the love of God, once and for all. If God be for me, who can be against me? Romans 8:31

The Bible says even if you lose mother and father, brothers and sisters, husbands and wives, houses and lands for the cause of the gospel, He'll give to you mothers and fathers, brothers and sisters, houses and lands a hundredfold in this life, and in the world to come, eternal life. Mark 10:29-30

So what's your problem? You say, "Well, Mama rejected me." Well, that is her problem; it is not your problem. It is her sin and you do not need to get into more sin over her sin. Who is true, your mama or God?

At some point, you are going to have to leave mother and father spiritually: mother and father, houses and lands. You are going to have to get back in the flow of eternity and know that you are a select individual. You have to accept that you are loved of God and you are eternally preserved for Him forever.

This planet was damned to sin because of your ancestral failure, but you do not have to continue the ancestral failure of your generations. Who do you want to get spiritual first, your mama or you? You want Mama to get spiritual, so then you will be healed. Come on, admit it. If Mama and Daddy would get it together, then you would not have a problem.

You are going to have to get to a place where you understand and believe that you are accepted of God and loved of God. When you get that settled in your heart, it will not make a difference what anyone ever says to you the rest of your life. They can spit in your face. They can do whatever they want, and you are so complete in the love of God that if anyone smiled at you today, it would just be a bonus to you.

It does not feel good when people burp all over you and reject you and say evil things to you. It is defiling, but get on with it. Do not take it inside yourself. Do not go there! That is their sin. Release them to their sin. Release yourself to God's blessings and provisions. Amen?

Let God be true and every man a liar... Romans 3:4 You have to settle that in your heart once and for all.

1 JOHN 4:18

> **There is no fear in love; but perfect love casteth out fear: because fear hath torment. He that feareth is not made perfect in love.** 1 John 4:18

Part I

There is no Fear in love

Well, if there is no Fear in love and you are complete in love, Fear has to go. If you are complete in God's love, why should you fear?

"Well, you do not know what they said about me. You do not know what they did to me."

Did God do that to you or did they do that to you? If they did it, then turn away from men and turn to God.

Get your eyes on God. Get your eyes on His love. What they did to you is so unimportant that 100 years from now, it will be the last thing on your mind. So if 100 years from now it will be the last thing on your mind, why are you making it so important in your life now? It is a non-eternal, futile effort to dwell on things that are not eternal.

Get your mind on things that are eternal, things that are above. Get your focus on what God has called you to in eternity, not what the devil has called you to.

"Well, if I take a stand for God, Mama might not like me."

Well, if Mama does not like you because you take a stand for God, that means Mama does not love God and that is her problem.

"But I am supposed to respect my parents."

You are supposed to respect your parents to the degree they respect God. Get it straight. Who are you following, your parents and their yucky puckies or God in His holiness? There is no Fear in love and right here we see the connection between love and Fear.

Your freedom depends on you, not on me. Are you able to mix this with your faith and get before God? Or are you just going to let it become knowledge for your head? Knowledge puffeth up, it is a vanity and it produces nothing. 1 Corinthians 8:1

But your faith mixed with knowledge can defeat devils all the way back to Satan himself. You need to be "madder than hell" with a godly anger because hell is mad at you.

This is a serious situation and your life is that important. There is no Fear in love, so if you want to get rid of Fear, let's cast it out.

Part II

Perfect love casts out Fear

First John tells you perfect love begins with the Godhead—with God, Jesus and the Holy Spirit. Be complete in them.

> 3**And every spirit that confesseth not that Jesus Christ is come in the flesh is not of God: and this is that *spirit* of antichrist, whereof ye have heard that it should come; and even now already is it in the world.**
>
> 4**Ye are of God, little children, and have overcome them: because greater is he that is in you, than he that is in the world.** 1 John 4:3-4

If you are waiting for some man to love you or some woman to love you so you will become complete, then you are in trouble. Those who will love you are going to die one day and then what are you going to do? You are stuck with yourself and all your problems.

You might as well get healed and well now. Get free of those Unloving spirits and that Bondage now while those who love you are alive. Be readying your faith because you are still going to have to live with yourself when they pass on. They are not eternal either.

> **Who are kept by the power of God through faith unto salvation ready to be revealed in the last time.** 1 Peter 1:5

So why should you go the way of hell? Why don't you go the way of heaven? Ignite a fire of resisting the devil inside your spirit.

Make a decision that you are going to walk in love, be loved, and that Fear is not going to be your guide. The Holy Spirit is the one who is your guide and the Word of God is your guide. No other father is your guide.

Who invited the devil to come and give his opinion? You did: "Satan, is that right? Do you think I need to believe that?" Then you have this discussion with the enemy. "Do you think this Fear thing is true?"

What is Fear going to tell you? "Nahhh!" What is that? Unbelief and Doubt.

One person came and died for you. It did not take an army. It took one man's love. One man's love sanctified creation forever. Hallelujah! Amen! He is the Bishop of my soul. If He is the Bishop of your soul, why are you listening to all those other voices?

He who knows the voice of the Good Shepherd, another voice he will not follow. John 10:16 Do you want to hear the voice of the Shepherd? Would you like Jesus to speak to you?

Here's what He would say to you, "Fear not. I am with you, even to the ends of the earth—to the end of the world." Matthew 28:20 Do you believe that? That is the voice of the Shepherd.

Another voice comes along and says, "Well, we will think about tomorrow... It is not going to go very well."

So the first thing you know, you have forgotten the voice of the Good Shepherd who says, "Be anxious for nothing, but in all things give thanks, for this is the will of God." Philippians 4:6

You forgot the voice of the Shepherd: "Peace give I unto you, not as the world gives give I unto you." John 14:27 You forgot the voice of the Shepherd. "I am the Shepherd." John 10:11

"The LORD is my Shepherd. He leadeth me beside still waters. He prepareth a table for me in the presence of my enemy." Psalm 23:1, 2, 5

When you walk into your home, which is ruled by that other kingdom, just take a good breath and look around and say, "Glory to God. I am the light of the world through Christ Jesus. Amen."

Part III

Fear hath torment

So if you are not perfect in the love of God and you have Fear within you, torment comes. It is torment of the spirit and torment of the soul. That is the mind-body connection.

Part IV

He that feareth is not made perfect in love

When you have Fear, you are not made perfect in love. You are unable to give and receive love without Fear: you do not know how to give love without Fear; and you cannot receive it without Fear.

Lack of love and the presence of Fear go hand-in-hand. If you know you are loved, Fear does not stand a chance. And if you do not feel you are loved, if you do not feel like you are accepted, Fear comes.

We look at our enemy, but we must keep our eyes on the Lord at the same time. Do not become overwhelmed by the things you see in your life. Keep your eyes on the Lord because He is Lord of all.

"Every knee shall bow, and every tongue shall confess that Jesus Christ is Lord." Romans 14:11 "The enemies of Christ shall be defeated, the last of which is death." 1 Corinthians15:26

He is Lord over disobedient spirits as well as obedient spirits. Even disobedient spirits will bow their knee one day to confess that He is Lord, to their shame. Philippians 2:10

Why go there in Shame? Why not go there in glory? You are going to believe God one day. Why not start believing Him now? "As for me and my house, we are going to serve the Lord." Amen? Joshua 24:15

Definitions of Fear

Definitions of fear from *Webster's Dictionary* include: a feeling or anxious thought; dread; expecting something unpleasant, often unknown or certain; alarm (fight or flight); fearful (as in full of fear, showing fear, the body language of fear).

There are fourteen different words that are translated into English for the word "fear" from Hebrew in the Old Testament and seven different words for "fear" from Greek in the New Testament.

One Hebrew word for "fear" is *tâvahh* (#8429 in the *Strong's Concordance*). The prime root means to be startled by a sudden alarm. When you are startled, it triggers the fight or flight reaction, which is part of creation. However, the fight or flight built into Fear projection is not a part of creation. Being startled *should* stimulate fight or flight. That is normal. It should have no long-term effect.

When you go across the road and you do not see a car coming, you are startled when someone beeps the horn. You jump back and say, "Oh, my! That was close!" Then you continue on with your journey in life and it is over with. That is what God created for you. Your mind-body connection is not evil.

Another Hebrew word for "fear" is *pachad* (#6342 in the *Strong's Concordance*), meaning to fear in general; to be afraid; to stand in awe; to be in fear; to make to shake. The neurological responses that produce shaking, trembling and even fibrillation problems in the heart all come out of anxiety and fear.

In the New Testament there are three Greek words used to translate the word "feared" and *#5399* accounts for 95 percent of them. It means to frighten; to be alarmed; or to revere. Another is *#2124* which is found in Hebrews 5:7. It means caution; reverence (piety); or dread.

Have you ever seen anyone with Fear in their eyes? I was ministering in a church in southern Maine in 1986, and the people brought an asthmatic woman to me. She was in the middle of an asthmatic attack. As they brought her to me, she dropped back on one knee and cowered as if she had seen the most evil thing in the world.

She was cowering in total Fear because the spirit producing asthma knew its days were over. When I ministered, that asthmatic attack stopped instantly. I cast the spirit out of her and she stood before us totally well.

At that time I did not know asthma was a result of a spirit of Fear, but now I know it well. Even the medical community has proven that asthma is not the result of anything you are exposed to, such as allergens, irritants or pollen. There is a mutant gene implicated in asthma which makes people more susceptible to allergies. We see asthma being inherited, especially in children.

Fear also involves a lot of body language. When that spirit behind asthma manifested, this woman acted like she had seen a ghost!

Another definition of fear is a fearmonger; a person who spreads fear and is a broker of fear. Have you ever been around people and all they do is speak negative fearful things? They are fearmongers.

Fear is also defined as fearsome, which means someone causing fear. The antonym is fearless, which means without fear and afraid of nothing.

What does the Word say? Be fearless! Be anxious for nothing. Be without fear.

To be without fear does not mean that you are not exposed to it. You can be totally without the spirit of Fear, yet still experience every emotion that would want to cause it to become part of your life.

TEMPTATION WITHOUT SIN

Is it possible for you to be tempted without sin? The Bible says, "Jesus was tempted in all points such as we are, yet without sin." Hebrews 5:14

Do you think that the spirit of Fear came to Jesus? If He was tempted in all points such as we are, it means He was exposed to everything you and I are exposed to, yet He did not bend to it. He did not let it come in and He did not let it be part of His life.

Many people have a mistaken concept that to be without fear means you are never exposed to it. They think if you are delivered from Fear, you will never have that feeling—you will never be around it again and never have to deal with it again. If you buy that, you have bought the biggest lie! That would mean Satan had been bound before his time.

There is a difference between Satan working through his kingdom and you having authority over him while he is still present. Satan will not be bound for a thousand years until the millennium.

Right now, he is on the loose with his whole kingdom and you have been given authority and power over him by the Word as a work of the Holy Spirit. Start taking your position in spite of him.

He wants you to be more afraid of him. Do you know he is more afraid of you than you are of him? Can I give you a scripture? "Resist the devil and he will flee." James 4:7 How fast is he going to flee? Well, if he does not flee instantly when you say so, you go into Fear.

The Bible says,

> **Wherefore take unto you the whole armour of God, that ye may be able to withstand in the evil day, and having done all, to stand.** Ephesians 6:13

You are eternal. The devil is not. He does not really want this battle. When I decide to flash my sword, those spirits do not stand a chance because they are more afraid of me than you can imagine. Why? Because I represent God, and they are afraid of God. They aren't afraid of me. They are afraid of God and me. Actually they *are* afraid of me because they know who is *with* me.

I do not come alone! Aren't you glad that we do not have to come alone? Amen!

"And it shall come to pass in the day that the Lord shall give thee rest from thy sorrow and from thy fear and from the hard bondage wherein thou wast made to serve." Isaiah 14:3

Do you think Fear is bondage? "God has not given you the spirit of bondage again to fear." Romans 8:15 The Word is going to deliver you from your sorrow, from your Fear and from your Bondage.

When you allow Fear to control you, sorrow comes with it. "Fear hath torment." The torment is in your mind and in your thoughts. Does that bring you sorrow? It brings you bondage. It brings you sorrow and it affects every aspect of your life. Fear will cause you to become phobic. Fear causes you to constantly set into motion a type of radar for other spirits to join it.

Have you ever watched radar screens and their constant "blip, blip, blip?" What are they showing? Obstacles in the pathway. Using this as a parable, radar or Fear can be the constant projection of danger.

But radar is not designed to *project* danger. Radar is set in place to discern things that are dangerous in your pathway. If you are not careful, you will come up with a faulty radar that is not looking for danger, but projecting it.

When you have the projection of danger in the future, you have torment. Discernment is a type of radar that gives you the ability to know good and evil.

Are we able to handle strong meat? A sign of maturity is when by reason of exercise of the senses, we are able to discern both good and evil. Hebrews 5:14 What does that mean?

You have radar going all the time. God's radar in you is discernment as a work of the Holy Spirit. One of the nine gifts of the Holy Spirit in 1 Corinthians 12 is discerning of spirits. How can you discern spirits when you cannot even see them? Well, sometimes you can see them pretty clearly in how people act and talk.

Now you need to replace the Fear projection with godly discernment. You can have discernment of everything that Fear represents and it still not have an effect on you. You are going to work it out in your life by practical application.

You are losing this battle right between your ears, so you need to take the battle right into the street. Take it right into your life. Walk right in the midst of it, and keep on moving. But Fear will not let you go there.

I talked to someone who said, "I just cannot leave my home. I cannot allow people to come in my home. They might bring something in."

I said, "Something is already there. What you have is worse than what others will bring. You need to get out of your home and take the stuff inside of you out of your home. Don't worry about what is coming in."

"Well, that is easy for you to say."

I said, "No, it isn't easy for me to say and it isn't easy for you to do. At some point you are going to have to start facing your enemy."

"Well, I might have a reaction."

"You're already having one just thinking about it."

"Well, I wonder why I'm not getting well."

I replied, "Because you will not dare face your enemy. You want your enemy to be defeated, you want the reaction to go away, and then you will say, 'Hey, I want to face my enemy.' Well, you take your reaction right with you and go face him."

PERSECUTION OR TRUTH?

There is also a Fear that someone could come against you. Jesus said they will persecute you until the day you die. So get used to it! Separate the person from their evil.

When you make the person evil, you have just been had. Take that into conviction and discernment for your own life. People do tell you the truth, even if sometimes in an evil way. You need to be honest with yourself and say, "Is this really something I need to deal with?"

Rather than taking it and sinning in Rejection, take it into wisdom. You must be able to face every issue and every person. Jesus said you would be persecuted.

Even King David said, "My enemies are my familiars." David said those closest to him were those who were damaging him. He ran to the LORD, his Creator. He ran to God for his fix.

The enemies of a man are his own household. Matthew 10:36 The battle is close to home. A prophet is without honor in his own country. John 4:44 Your battleground is with those closest to you, not some stranger in the street.

It is so intense because you have a need to be loved. So get back with your Father in heaven. If you are waiting for the world and your family to love you in every area, you are going to be waiting for a long time. It may never happen. Just get on with your life and keep a right spirit within you.

David said,

> **Create in me a clean heart, O God; and renew a right spirit within me.** Psalm 51:10

Someone has to get spiritual here. Who is it going to be? You are the one who has to work out your own salvation daily. Philippians 2:12 You are the one who has to come before God and accept His love. You are the one who has to understand the nature of the war going on in this planet. You are the one who has to have spiritual discernment. You are the one who has to be a man or woman of God.

Get on with who you are. You have to become eternal in your thinking. This life is fleeting and passing. You have

70 to 80, maybe 90 years, and then you are going to be like the flower that fades and blows away.

> **The days of our years *are* threescore years and ten; and if by reason of strength *they be* fourscore years, yet *is* their strength labour and sorrow; for it is soon cut off, and we fly away.** Psalm 90:10

> **For he knoweth our frame; he remembereth that we *are* dust. *As for* man, his days *are* as grass: as a flower of the field, so he flourisheth. For the wind passeth over it, and it is gone; and the place thereof shall know it no more.** Psalm 103:14-16

Make sure you have part in the first resurrection. The Bible says he that hath part in the first resurrection shall not face the second death.

> **Blessed and holy *is* he that hath part in the first resurrection: on such the second death hath no power, but they shall be priests of God and of Christ, and shall reign with him a thousand years.** Revelation 20:6

Make sure you are right with God. Let no man be your God and let no man be your guide. Let God be your guide. Let God be your Word. Let God be your standard and keep your eyes on Him and what He has said about you.

He says you are fearfully and wonderfully made and before He ever fashioned your bones and eyeballs and all your parts, He knew you.

> **14I will praise thee; for I am fearfully *and* wonderfully made: marvellous *are* thy works; and *that* my soul knoweth right well.**

> **15My substance was not hid from thee, when I was made in secret, *and* curiously wrought in the lowest parts of the earth.**

> **16Thine eyes did see my substance, yet being unperfect; and in thy book all *my members* were written, *which* in**

continuance were fashioned, when *as yet there was* none of them. Psalm 139:14-16

You are engraved on the palms of His hands.

Behold, I have graven thee upon the palms of *my* hands; thy walls *are* continually before me. Isaiah 49:16

In the genetics of mankind, you are no accident and you are going to have to accept that once and for all.

Jeremiah says,

For thus saith the LORD; We have heard a voice of trembling, of fear, and not of peace. Jeremiah 30:5

When you speak, is it coming out as a voice of fear and trembling? "What if" is the number one statement of Fear. But wisdom is certain. Wisdom says, "This is it." Wisdom says, "When." Knowledge takes you from the past to the present, but wisdom takes you from the present to the future. We want to make sure that when you have knowledge, it is not Fear taking you into the future.

It says in Proverbs,

Wisdom...uttereth her voice in the streets: Proverbs 1:20

Are you listening to her? Fear is crying in the streets. Are you listening to him? Whose voice are you following?

The Bible says,

There are, it may be, so many kinds of voices in the world, and none of them *is* without signification.
1 Corinthians 14:10

So many voices demand that you listen. There are Pied Pipers all over the place saying, "Follow me, follow me, follow me." The Bible says in the Psalms,

Thy word *is* a lamp unto my feet, and a light unto my path. Psalm 119:105

The Holy Spirit shall lead you into all truth.

Howbeit when he, the Spirit of truth, is come, he will guide you into all truth: for he shall not speak of himself; but whatsoever he shall hear, *that* shall he speak: and he will shew you things to come. John 16:13

Drivenness is of the devil, but leadership is of God. You must learn to discern the voices talking within you.

Mark says,

35 And the same day, when the even was come, he saith unto them, Let us pass over unto the other side.

36 And when they had sent away the multitude, they took him even as he was in the ship. And there were also with him other little ships.

37 And there arose a great storm of wind, and the waves beat into the ship, so that it was now full.

38 And he was in the hinder part of the ship, asleep on a pillow: and they awake him, and say unto him, Master, carest thou not that we perish?

39 And he arose, and rebuked the wind, and said unto the sea, Peace, be still. And the wind ceased, and there was a great calm.

40 And he said unto them, Why are ye so fearful? how is it that ye have no faith?

41 And they feared exceedingly, and said one to another, What manner of man is this, that even the wind and the sea obey him? Mark 4:35-41

What did they have their eyes on? Dying. They had Fear of dying and Fear of Death. What is the worst thing that could have happened to them? They could have died and gone to paradise and then they would have been taken to heaven right after Christ rose from the dead.

A good teaching on dealing with Fear is when Paul was a prisoner in the ship that was about to sink. What happened with him? The great wisdom and Spirit of God came on him in the face of death—and it was not just for himself, but for all the Gentile heathens on the ship. Read that in Acts 27 and you will see a great victory.

And Jesus arose and He rebuked the wind. What did He do with Fear? Rebuked it. He said, "Get behind me, Satan. I resist you!" Matthew 4:10

What did his faith do? It confronted Fear. "Faith is the substance of things hoped for, the evidence not yet seen." Hebrews 11:1

In the Book of Henry, it goes like this: "Fear is the substance of things not hoped for, the evidence not yet seen." "Fear and faith are equal in this dimension: They both demand to be fulfilled. "

"According to your fear, so be it unto you." Matthew 9:29 Job said, "The thing that I greatly feared has come upon me." Job 3:25 Fear has a fruit. When confronted with the fear and confronted with the possibility of destruction Jesus rebuked the wind and said unto the sea, "Peace."

They were confronted with what Fear represented. What did the disciples say? "We are going to die!"

What did Jesus say? "We are going to live."

Jesus did not yield to Fear. He took authority over what was behind the storm, which was the devil. Satan is called the prince of the power of the air.

Wherein in time past ye walked according to the course of this world, according to the prince of the power of the air, the spirit that now worketh in the children of disobedience:
Ephesians 2:2

So right in the beginning of the stages of Fear, behind the storm, there was an invisible force. When Jesus rebuked the sea, He was rebuking the force causing it. When the force was broken, guess what happened to the winds? They were gone just like that!

Do you know that you have the same ability to deal with your enemy if you just believe? Start practicing it.

Fear is a spirit. It controls you by programming your mind and your memes to Fear. You have been programmed in your generations to be fearful, not just from a spiritual standpoint, but from a soulish standpoint.

How do you develop new ways of thinking? By practicing them.

This is not mind over matter. This is a practical application. Your mind is renewed by the washing of the water of the Word. Ephesians 5:26 You meditate on the Word of God day and night.

What does that mean? By meditating on the Word of God day and night you are establishing new memes based on what God said. Break an old habit by creating new ones. If you have a bad habit of being afraid, develop a new habit of believing by repetitious application. Start defeating your enemy. Go out and face him on a repetitive basis.

He rebuked the sea, "Peace, be still." The wind ceased, and there was a great calm. Jesus said unto them, "Why are you so fearful?" Mark 4:40

You may say, "Pastor, it is natural to be afraid."

Yes, it is, but because it is natural to be concerned about some things does not mean we have to step into Satan's dimension. What is the worst thing that could have happened to them? They could have died and gone to paradise.

Was this a situation that involved fight or flight? Yes. Was it possible for the boat to sink? Yes. Jesus confronted them and said, "Why are you so fearful? How is it that you have no faith?"

What is the opposite of Fear? What is the opposite of faith? Here you see the comparison of fear and faith being equal. They were expecting fear to be fulfilled. Jesus was expecting faith to be fulfilled.

"And they feared exceedingly…" Mark 4:41 What kind of Fear do they have now? They are afraid of Jesus. The sea is already calm.

Mark 4:41 uses *Strong's #5401,* which is found only one time in the New Testament. It is used specifically in this instance to mean "alarmed, or to be put in fear."

Now, is alarmed the same thing as the fruit of being alarmed? No, this is a situation where Jesus has just gotten their attention and they realize He is more than what they thought He was. This is why it is so important to do word studies. If you weren't careful, you might make this word the evil form of fear, which it is not.

And they feared exceedingly and said to one another, "What manner of man is this?" They were in awe of what He could do next to them. They thought, "If this man has this kind of power over the sea, what could He do to us in our fear? The wind and the sea obey Him, but we do not always obey Him!"

Now if the wind and sea obey the Lord, what do you think we should do? We need to have a reverential fear and respect for the God we serve and Who saved us. He has told us not to fear. We need to have a reverential respect and fear of the Lord—so would you obey Him and get out of your Fears? This is a life circumstance that Jesus dealt with.

The disciples were confronted with an issue. The winds and the seas obeyed Him, but they did not obey Him in peace. Fear is disobedience to God. Fear is a sin.

Did Jesus say you would not be confronted with Fear? No. Did He ever say you would not be exposed to it? No. Did He ever tell say you would not be rejected? No.

Did Jesus tell you that you would always be loved and never rejected? Did He ever tell you that everyone would love you, accept you, care for you and say wonderful things to you? Did He ever tell you no one would curse you?

He told you none of those things. He said you would be persecuted in all manners. He was telling you there is evil in the world and you would be subjected to it. But that does not mean it has to go into you and become part of your life.

On the right hand of God you have been raised up, seated in heavenly places with Christ Jesus far above all principalities and powers.

> [20]**Which he wrought in Christ, when he raised him from the dead, and set *him* at his own right hand in the heavenly *places*,**
>
> [21]**Far above all principality, and power, and might, and dominion, and every name that is named, not only in this world, but also in that which is to come:** Ephesians 1:20-21

Knowing that he which raised up the Lord Jesus shall raise up us also by Jesus, and shall present *us* with you.
2 Corinthians 4:14

Fear is a principality and a power.

14For as many as are led by the Spirit of God, they are the sons of God.

15For ye have not received the spirit of bondage again to fear; but ye have received the Spirit of adoption, whereby we cry, Abba, Father.

16The Spirit itself beareth witness with our spirit, that we are the children of God:

17And if children, then heirs; heirs of God, and joint-heirs with Christ; if so be that we suffer with *him,* that we may be also glorified together. Romans 8:14-17

For God hath not given us the spirit of fear; but of power, and of love, and of a sound mind. 2 Timothy 1:7

God has not given you a spirit of Bondage again to Fear, but power, love and a sound mind. But He has also given you something else, the "Abba, Father." Romans 8:15

We have not been given a spirit of Bondage again to Fear, but the Spirit of adoption. Adoption means you are loved. Adoption means they want to give you their name. This is a little different than being a foster child. Adoption means you get my name. You are my son; you are my daughter, just as if I were your biological father.

The term "blood is thicker than water" means you are bound to the iniquity of your ancestry—and that is not necessarily good! It means your ancestral curses are going to rule and you are going to take the side of your parents even if they are evil.

I do not agree with that. God does not agree with that because He said you shall leave mother and father, houses and lands, because of the gospel. Jesus does not believe "blood is thicker than water." He thinks God is greater than any blood of man. The blood of Jesus Christ is greater than the blood of men. Amen?

Are you getting my point? You say, "What does this have to do with Fear?" It has to do with establishing a foundation for your thinking. You cannot defeat Fear if you don't have faith. How are you going to get faith? By hearing. And what are you going to be hearing? The Word of God. Now tuck it away in your heart. Let not your heart be troubled but put your trust in God.

Take this in and make it part of your nature. Do not let Fear touch you again. It may be all over you, but you are not going to take it inside yourself. The Bible says the evil one came to Christ and found nothing within Him.

> **Hereafter I will not talk much with you: for the prince of this world cometh, and hath nothing in me.** John 14:30

If an evil spirit is trying to link up with you and give you its nature, you need to remove the part of you that allows it in. So when it comes to try you, it finds nothing within you. Amen?

Disease Prevention

Wouldn't you like to prevent many of the diseases that are coming from anxiety and Self-Hatred? Wouldn't you like to be free, in advance? Wouldn't it be nice to get to heaven one day and hear the Lord say, "You listened to what Pastor taught you, and you lived out your days to be a good, ripe old age.

"There were five diseases that would have killed you prematurely—or made your life miserable until death—and you did not get them because I was able to meet you. You did not get sick and I want you to know that that was my blessing." Wouldn't it be wonderful to know that was part of God's blessing to you?

Do not take God for granted, and do not just concentrate on the things that are not resolved in your life. But give thanks to God for the things that are accomplished in your life! If you do not have the diseases that you could have had, give Him thanks! Thank Him for keeping you from it.

I thank God every day for my health. I thank God every day for being my Father. I thank God every day for increasing me in knowledge and stature so that I can apply my heart to righteousness—because I know it is good for my health and it is good for my relationship with Him, with myself and with others.

Luke says,

> **25 And there shall be signs in the sun, and in the moon, and in the stars; and upon the earth distress of nations, with perplexity; the sea and the waves roaring;**

> **26 Men's hearts failing them for fear, and for looking after those things which are coming on the earth: for the powers of heaven shall be shaken.** Luke 21:25-26

So men's hearts are failing them for Fear. Do you know how many people die in earthquakes that did not get killed by the earthquake, but died of a heart attack because of Fear? They survived the earthquake, yet they died because of Fear.

Fear can kill you. Fear can produce many problems. The very thing that produces a heart attack in sudden fight or flight—or the Alarm Stage of the natural tragedy around you—long-term, can do the same thing to you. It's just a slow death rather than a quick one.

If you have any indication of heart disease in your family tree, especially down from your father or your mother's father, make a list of things to deal with and put Fear on it. Not only do you need to deal with it, you need to deal with the genetics that produced it.

Genetics can be changed as a creative miracle through prayer

The term "butterflies in my chest" is a manifestation of Fear and anxiety. Did you ever have to get up and stand before someone and speak or sing, and you became really nervous? I think everyone deals with that to some degree. Most everyone has a certain amount of Fear of man, Fear of Failure and Fear of Rejection.

Because those forces come to attack you in certain situations, it does not mean you have to yield to them. You know you can stand with those butterflies in your chest hammering through you. You can come with the Spirit of God within you, speaking through you.

> [11]**And when they bring you unto the synagogues, and** ***unto*** **magistrates, and powers, take ye no thought how or what thing ye shall answer, or what ye shall say:**
>
> [12]**For the Holy Ghost shall teach you in the same hour what ye ought to say.** Luke 12:11-12

RELATIONSHIPS

Do you freeze when you come against someone you fear? Do you have difficulty presenting yourself before others without Fear, sometimes even in simple conversation? Do you have difficulty dealing with a family member who, the minute you show your face, is already attacking you verbally?

I read an article in the *Atlanta Journal-Constitution* written by a Jewish staff member. It was describing his relationship with his deceased loved one. This man was separated from his father and did not believe in heaven, or hell, or deity, or God, or even life after death. He was a Sadducee.

He said that every time he got around his father it was just a constant barrage, "Do this. Don't do this. What are you doing? You're not taking care of your life properly. You're not succeeding. You're not this; you're not that."

Finally he stayed away from his father for years and, when he called him once a year, it would be the same thing all over again—a bombardment of Accusation.

He figured his father just hated him. His father died and he never had peace with him. He went through his father's things after his death. His father had recorded every phone conversation, every letter that had been written and had kept a diary of his love for his son.

He hung on every word his son said and yearned for every moment with him, but when he would get with his son, he would just slay him with his mouth. That man had to deal with the issue that his father loved him, but never could show it. Now that is a tragedy. That is one of the greatest tragedies I have ever read in my life.

These are spiritual issues. The Bible says out of your mouth come blessings and cursings and this should not be. How is it that from the same fountain can come sweet water and bitter water? Let your yeas be yeas and your nays be nays. Out of your mouth should not come cursing and blessing.

> **10 Out of the same mouth proceedeth blessing and cursing. My brethren, these things ought not so to be.**
>
> **11 Doth a fountain send forth at the same place sweet *water* and bitter?** James 3:10-11

> **But above all things, my brethren, swear not, neither by heaven, neither by the earth, neither by any other oath: but let your yea be yea; and *your* nay, nay; lest ye fall into condemnation.** James 5:12

It is a spiritual problem. The father cared but his way of showing it was a constant barrage of accusation. He made his son feel like he had blown it in every area of life. This Jewish father never took time to show his son the God of Abraham, Isaac and Jacob. The son was an atheist.

Well, how do you handle this? If at all possible, be able to talk about problems. I think we ought to require responsibility in relationship. It is hard when it is family, isn't it? It is hard when every time that family member opens his mouth, he attacks you verbally.

At some point you just have to get away from it. I go to the Word. "If at all possible, live peaceably one with another." Romans 12:18 "Mark those that cause division and have no part with them." Romans 16:17 The Bible also says to leave mother and father, husbands and wives, houses and lands for the cause of the gospel. Mark 10:29-30

Standing for God's Word in peace in your relationships is part of the gospel. Do you think you can take a stand for righteousness against an evil person and not have a bad attitude yourself? And not sin? Do you think you have to repay evil for evil?

Do you think when people are blowing you away with their tongue you have to come back and do the same thing? When you do, you have lost the covering of God and you have opened the door for the devil in every area.

James says where there is strife, there is every evil thing and if you cannot say something good, don't say anything at all.

> **For where envying and strife *is*, there *is* confusion and every evil work.** James 3:16

> **Speak not evil one of another, brethren. He that speaketh evil of *his* brother, and judgeth his brother, speaketh evil of the law, and judgeth the law: but if thou judge the law, thou art not a doer of the law, but a judge.** James 4:11

Can you stand there and keep your mouth shut? With everything raging in your ears and your mind and the programmed memes from past Rejection? Can you stand there in the peace of God?

This is an unperfected area of spirituality in every Christian's life. When Jesus was being persecuted, spit upon and scourged, He still held His peace. He did not defend

Himself. When they would say something to Him, true or not, He would simply say, "This is what *you* say. So be it."

He never defended Himself. He never spit back fire. He could have called down 10,000 angels. He could have slain every single one of them. He could have destroyed this planet with a spoken word. He had the power.

But Jesus simply said, as He was giving up the ghost, "Father, forgive them. They know not what they are doing." Luke 23:24

What was He saying? They were spiritually insane. Are you able to stand before someone who is spiritually insane and keep your sanity? Do you know when people are spouting off evil to you that they are spiritually insane at that moment? Are you able to be like your Lord and hold your peace?

He was able to stand before them without Fear because He knew the will of God. So we do not stand before a person and hold our peace because we know the conclusion of the matter. We hold our peace because that is our peace, not our Fear. Jesus did not defend Himself.

The Bible says that He had done nothing wrong. In fact, Pilate said, "I find no fault with this man. He is not guilty." John 19:6 Basically, Pilate said to the crowd, "You are guilty. You are the murderers. He is not guilty. I find no fault in Him."

The Bible says Jesus was without sin. Hebrews 4:15 Jesus did not defend Himself even in His righteousness.

When someone is attacking you and you are not guilty, you have a tendency to want to defend yourself in your righteousness. You want to convince that person you are okay, but you are wasting your time. They are not interested in your righteousness. They are interested in your destruction and their exaltation.

The Bible says, "Reprove not a scorner..." Proverbs 9:8 My interpretation is, "Reprove not a scorner because he is going to eat you for lunch!"

I have often seen people who were innocent try to defend themselves and try to insert the goodness of who they are in their thinking. Every word they said would be turned against them and made evil. I have never seen one person win a verbal battle. Both lose.

Hold your peace. There is nothing that infuriates a spirit speaking through a person more than for you to hold your peace. It will do and say whatever it has to do and say to get you to respond and feed its thought process.

It will goad you. It will slander you. It will mock you. It will do whatever it can to get you to respond. It will call you a wimp. It will tell you that you don't care because you're not saying anything back. It will say whatever is necessary to get you into the flesh and open your mouth.

The victory in this one is to hold your peace and stare right at it. Just let it shoot off until it is finished, then it has no more to say except the same thing over again. After a while it runs out of steam, but you have not said anything that it can feed on and turn against you.

At some point, if you have to, rather than be a victim of it forever, you will simply say, "When we can have a conversation that is peaceable, we will resume. If not, there will be none." Then walk away. The Bible says, "If at all possible, live peaceably one with another."

I was teaching a few years ago in a session where an unsaved individual confronted me. He rose up against me, openly challenged me and took over my whole seminar. All I could do was just stand there and go back and forth and keep a right spirit. How I handled that individual won many people to the Lord and eventually won him to the Lord. Today he is saved. It was over a truth issue and it could have gone either way.

Jesus was dealing with a truth issue; He was not dealing with any other area. When they would come against Him physically in His ministry to destroy Him or to stone Him, He would pass through them and keep on going. He just moved away from them because there was no more dialogue. To the degree that He could teach, He taught. When He couldn't, He moved on.

We see the very nature of that in how He taught the disciples in Matthew, Mark, Luke and John. He said, "When you go into a house, if you can leave your peace in the house, stay. If you cannot, then move on." Matthew 10:13-14

If you cannot leave your peace in the home you are staying in, kick the dust off your feet and keep on moving. It shall be worse for that house in the day of judgment than it was for Sodom and Gomorrah, because you came bearing gifts of peace and truth and it was not received.

So what do you do? You say, "Have a nice day. I sure love you," and move on.

SPIRITUAL DISCERNMENT

If people are obviously trying to "get your goat" and goading you, say nothing. You know who you are and you know you are going to have a new body in the resurrection. If you bump into people who want to injure—people who speak demeaning things designed to hurt and control, remember Psalm 139. The Word says you are fearfully and wonderfully made. Know who you are.

First of all, these people are not your friends. And second, they have a wrong spirit. What you might say to get out of this is, "Well, thank you for your opinion and your insight. Thank you for your concern." Then move on, because if you don't, you are going to be opened up for dialogue and there is a spirit in them that wants to destroy.

If you move away and there is something happening inside you, then you have spirits of Rejection, Unloving or Fear that need to be recognized. If there is residue and it does not go away but starts to torment you, there is something within you that needs to be dealt with.

The spirit that was in them knew the spirit that was in you and knew just what to say to link up with the spirit in you. Now it is time for you to have discernment.

You may say, "I have a spiritual problem. What they said was designed to stir that thing up on the inside of me. Now I'm going to recognize and take responsibility for it."

We are dealing with an invisible kingdom of beings that know each other and can see each other. The spirit in that person knows the one in you and they know how to make you a victim. That is the first lesson of discernment.

Now you can be defiled by it and still take your peace. But if you walk away and over a period of days and weeks that thing is still there, then you have a spirit of Rejection or Victimization. You have an Unloving spirit that needs to be dealt with.

MARRIAGE

Linking Spirits

If you have a spirit of Fear, there is a spirit in another person looking for you as a victim. It is the same type of spiritual linking that takes a woman away from her abusive father into a marriage with an abusive husband. She does not see it coming until after the marriage and he starts the victimization.

The first thing she says is, "I can't believe I married my father." There was a spirit of Victimization in her that was not dealt with and there was a spirit in that husband-to-be. Those spirits knew each other. They knew how to bring the relationship into a place of marriage, so they could gain control and fulfill themselves in the act of victimization.

Family Tree

That is why it is important to look at family trees. In fact, one of the first things you may want to do if you plan to get married is to sit down and do a family tree. Look at all the areas that could trip up your relationship. You are a child of God and have discernment. Look at your family tree. Look at your personal lives and those areas that would be shaky, then come before God and deal with it.

If you do not do this, it will be carried over into the marriage. It is a fact of life. Do you have Fear of getting married? Do you have Fear of relationships? No, now you have wisdom. Now you have discernment. If someone really loves you, he or she will not have a problem dealing with his or her life. When you are married, you become one flesh.

That does not mean you bring a whole bunch of stuff with you. You take it and set it aside.

Remember that Fear not only controls you spiritually, but also through the memes in your mind. You have been programmed to fear. You are going to have to be able to walk out of your programming.

Relationship

Couples going into a marriage relationship should be very honest with each other and become very transparent in dealing with those areas. If someone does not want to deal with it beforehand, the person will not deal with it after marriage either.

Many unsaved men try to get good Christian wives, because there is a beautiful thing about a godly woman. An evil man who has that spirit in him wants to victimize every good woman.

We are supposed to be the body of Christ. There is something else called the body of sin in the earth. It's time for discernment.

> **Knowing this, that our old man is crucified with *him*, that the body of sin might be destroyed, that henceforth we should not serve sin.** Romans 6:6

I have seen many men seek out a woman, go to church with her, go through all the acts, but never make a commitment to God. She says, "Well, when I marry him…"

Or he will say, "When we get married, we'll go to church." But when the knot is tied, the best that can be had is good intentions and the rest is downhill because of the fall of man and the evil that is in mankind.

Some people can be very critical toward you. I am not talking about casual contact with evil people who defile you. I am talking about being in relationships with people who are evil to you, like someone in your family. Relationship involves a two-way street.

In your relationships you should be able to stand against evil, not in silence, but in dialogue with a right attitude. I am not talking about when someone is attacking you viciously. I am talking about people with whom we are supposed to be in relationship.

If I cross the line with conduct towards my wife, I would expect her to confront me, not go silent. Why? Because we are in relationship. Now there are casual acquaintances. There are also people who victimize others as a way of life, but it does not have to be this way in your family.

If people say they want to be in relationship with you—and you want to be in relationship with them—then you should have an honest dialogue of righteousness at all times. That is what *koinonia,* the Greek word for fellowship, is all about.

If people do not conduct themselves properly, the Bible says mark those who cause division and have no part with them. At some point you have to come to a place, if you are going to be in relationship, where you do not allow this to continue to happen. It is injuring you and you cannot keep being injured.

If they really love you and they really want to be in relationship with you, they need to conduct themselves differently. If not, you are going to have to withdraw. That is your choice. If people cop an attitude in their Rejection, withdraw. That is the best you can do. Jesus withdrew.

We are trying to give you some little bits and pieces to help you meet all the different situations in life. There is enough information in the Scriptures to help you get through it all and of course the Holy Spirit can help you.

Many people have attacked me, but I have taken my time and held my ground in peace. I did not confront them, but continued to talk to them, got past the issues and won their hearts. Later, because we then had a better relationship, we were able to work out the other problems.

Do not always think you have to become legalistic and take the Word and run with it. The Word is there to give you a foundation, but wisdom is as important as knowledge. Knowledge will take you to understanding, but wisdom will help you bridge it. So let's take some time.

The Holy Spirit can give wisdom, but the point we are trying to make concerns *situational* victimization, not *continual* victimization. You can have a bad day and just blow it. That is situational victimization. That can be repented of and dealt with.

If a person does not take responsibility and repent for sin, he will do it again, and again, and again until it is broken. You need to be really aware of people who repent, do the same thing and repent again. Now I know Jesus says to forgive them 70 times seven. Yes, you do that, but after a point, if it is a continual rollover, deal with it.

Good intentions do not count. A guy who beats up on his wife can come back to repent, saying, "I am not going to do it again," but until that thing is dealt with in his life, it will happen again. Evil men want godly women.

The Holy Spirit can protect a godly woman unless there is something within her that has not been dealt with. I have seen many godly women who had abuse in their family trees. Even though she is a godly woman, she really should be going before God to get this problem checked out. She really should be paying attention to what that man is doing.

Just because a warm body is attracted to you does not mean it is from God. We have such a strong need to be loved! The big thing you hear is this, "Gals, get a good one while you can because life's too short."

There is such a pressure by families on women today to be married. It is incredible. They say, "You are not a whole person unless you have a man. You are not desirable."

Sometimes Fear drives us into relationship because of our need to be loved. Marriage should come out of long-term fellowship and relationship when you know who you are together. An evil spirit, if one is there, will always manifest. And it will manifest before marriage if you give it enough time, but people tend to run into marriage too quickly.

In the Jewish tradition when the man came to the woman and betrothed her, it was as if they were married even though it was two years before they actually got married. When they did get married, he got a year off from his job. They had that time to be together before he had to go back to work.

When there was war, he did not have to go. Yea, God! You know us really well! What a honeymoon! One year long! If there was war, you did not have to be a draft dodger. You got pardoned automatically, because you could party with that woman for one year. Yeah, God! Don't you love Him? What a Daddy!

Man ruined God's plan for a year-long honeymoon. I can see it now, a man getting married goes up to his boss, and says, "I'm getting married. I want the next year off with pay. I want to party with that girl for one year."

If we did that we'd have some wonderful marriages. Amen? Yeah, God! What a way to go!

As a pastor, I'd preach it. I'd go to that boss and say, "I want one year off just to get to know that woman. I will be a better employee when I get back. I promise you will have fewer problems to worry about."

Save up enough money, let the family get together and take care of your needs the next year. You just go party together. Glory to God!

Thought and Words

Sometimes we need to build time between the thought and the words that form on the end of the tongue. If we take an hour to get the next sentence out, we might be better off.

I can see it now. Someone says something bad to you, and you are waiting for the Holy Spirit to speak through you. You stand there staring at them. "Well, what have you got to say? Hurry up!"

You say, "Just a minute."

Luke says, "And when they bring you unto the synagogues, and *unto* magistrates, and powers, take ye no thought how or what thing ye shall answer, or what ye shall say." Luke 12:11 Sometimes you need to count to ten between the thought and the words. Sometimes there is a spirit in you that wants to speak through you just like that. Why don't you give the Holy Spirit a chance?

Do you think this only applies when you are taken before the magistrate and powers because of the gospel? I am sure the scripture is designed for that, but I think the spiritual application is that we need to build a gap between thought and speech.

When you come up before people, hold your peace. If the Holy Spirit cannot get a word in edgewise, what is He going to do for you? He is going to back off and you are going to fall into the pit. He is going to have to dig you back out again.

Let's build in some time. We run off at the mouth because we are running off at the brain. If we speak without thinking, we are in real trouble. Speech without thought provides an open, fertile ground for an evil spirit.

When we speak too fast and we are out of control with our mouths, it is not us speaking anymore. You know it is not the Holy Ghost speaking because of the destruction that comes out from behind it. Your words will tell which kingdom you are establishing: the kingdom of God or the kingdom of the devil.

The Bible says,

> **...every idle word that men shall speak, they shall give account thereof in the day of judgment.** Matthew 12:36

What do we do immediately? We still have words out there that demand fulfillment. The Bible says your tongue, your words, are either life or death.

> **Death and life *are* in the power of the tongue: and they that love it shall eat the fruit thereof.** Proverbs 18:21

What you say demands to be fulfilled. Not that your Fear or faith demand to be fulfilled—but what you say demands to be fulfilled. If you say you hate yourself, then that demands to be fulfilled. All the autoimmune diseases come because you hate yourself.

Your words demand fulfillment. As *you* attack *yourself* spiritually and verbally, your *body* will eventually attack *itself,* because you forced it to come into agreement. There are consequences to sin; the wages of sin are death, both spiritual and physical. Premature death is a curse.

Every word you say will be held against you in judgment. Matthew 12:36 The Unloving spirit will not remind us God said, "We are the apple of His eye." Deuteronomy 32:10 We are the best thing since peanut butter. We need to remind ourselves of what God has said about us so we don't sin against God.

> **Thy word have I hid in mine heart, that I might not sin against thee.**
> Psalm 119:11

In John 6:51, we read that the Word of God is to be made flesh to our flesh. This means the very thing we take in from the Word of God, what we believe and tuck away in our heart, is made part of our spiritual consciousness and our soul consciousness as a way of life and shall bear the fruit of it.

It is not what we say first, it is what we believe. With the heart man believeth unto righteousness. Then confession is made unto salvation.

> **For with the heart man believeth unto righteousness; and with the mouth confession is made unto salvation.**
> Romans 10:10

It is not the confession! I heard someone say the other day, "If you confess this scripture three times a day, morning, noon and night, then you shall be well." That is witchcraft. That is a mantra.

It is not what you confess; it is what you believe in your heart. From what you believe in your heart, then confession is made unto salvation; otherwise it will not produce anything. Just believe it in your heart. I do not care what thoughts come to me against the Word of God, I cast them down as a vain imagination, holding every thought in captivity.

> **Casting down imaginations, and every high thing that exalteth itself against the knowledge of God, and bringing into captivity every thought to the obedience of Christ;**
> 2 Corinthians 10:5

I believe it whether I understand it or not. I believe God's Word! It is not an intellectual thing. We become one with what He said. Jesus is the Word.

If I have the mind of Christ, what does that mean? I am everything He said about me and I believe it.

There is a difference between meditation and vain repetition. If you believe in your heart, "I am the apple of God's eye," it is now part of your spiritual existence. That is godly meditation, but there is also a counterfeit. If you are trying to force it into yourself, then it is vain repetition. If you are confessing it because you believe it, that is meditation—you are repeating it out of the integrity of your heart.

Meditation
is confessing the Word
because you believe it

David said, "Let the meditations of my heart be acceptable to You."

> **Let the words of my mouth, and the meditation of my heart, be acceptable in thy sight, O LORD, my strength, and my redeemer.**
> Psalm 19:14

The meditations of my heart are what I believe and who I am: the expression from within myself. But if you are trying to bring it inside from without (outside yourself), that is wrong. It just takes one time for you to believe it. You just believe it.

When I read that I was the apple of God's eye, that I was engraved on the palms of His hands, that He loved me from the foundation of the world, that I was created from the foundation of the world, that the hairs of my head are numbered, I tucked that away in my heart. Psalm 17:8, Isaiah 49:16, Ephesians 1:4-5, Matthew 10:30

When the devil comes and says, "You're just this podunk nobody," I say, "Well, that's what you say. But let me remind you of what my Father said about me. I am not who I shall be. From glory to glory I am being changed." I just remind my enemy of who I am. It's not a mantra, nor is it a vain repetition. That is who I am by faith. 1 John 3:2, 2 Corinthians 3:18

I am not who I shall be

Is there anything wrong with hanging declarations on your refrigerators? No. Is there anything wrong with repeating it? No. But there is something wrong if people tell you to do that. They should also tell you to not become one with it. Many times it is not taught that way.

Some say, "If you do thus and such, then God will honor it." No, God only honors your faith as you mix it with the Word. He does not honor the Word by itself. He honors the Word when you mix your faith with it.

The Pharisees had the Word of God, but their hearts were far from God. They quoted the Word to Jesus, but the *letter* of the law kills. The *spirit* of the law brings life. 2 Corinthians 3:6 Is the law (the Word) the same under the letter as it is under the spirit? One is for death and destruction and one is for salvation and life. Both are based on the same Word of God.

Go to the Scriptures to become one with God, not because you want anything from Him. Become one with Him in His nature. That is who you have been created to be. You have your uniqueness, but it still is according to His nature.

Matthew says,

> **Either make the tree good, and his fruit good; or else make the tree corrupt, and his fruit corrupt: for the tree is known by *his* fruit.** Matthew 12:33

In another scripture it talks about the same fountain spouting out blessings one moment and cursings the next.

> **Out of the same mouth proceedeth blessing and cursing. My brethren, these things ought not so to be.** James 3:10

Do you know how many Christians are being evil one moment and then good the next? Forget about Christians. What about the world? Wouldn't it be awful to go to your tap to get a drink of water if it was salt water one moment and then fresh water the next—if it was bitter then sweet? We are either giving good fruit or bad fruit.

"Now look here, generation of vipers..." He called them snakes. "How can you, being evil, speak good things. For out of the abundance of the heart the mouth speaks." Matthew 12:34 "For as a man thinks in his heart, so is he." Prov.erbs 23:7

When people are coming against you, the very evil they are promoting is within them. If a person says that you have a big nose, they really have a bigger one and do not want you to know it. They may like your nose, but Envy and Jealousy is saying, "Ha! Let's put that nose down!" Envy and Jealousy puts down the things it really likes.

Luke says,

> **A good man out of the good treasure of his heart bringeth forth that which is good; and an evil man out of the evil treasure of his heart bringeth forth that which is evil: for of the abundance of the heart his mouth speaketh.** Luke 6:45

Matthew says,

> **[36]But I say unto you, That every idle word that men shall speak, they shall give account thereof in the day of judgment.**
>
> **[37]For by thy words thou shalt be justified, and by thy words thou shalt be condemned.** Matthew 12:36-37

The Greek word *argos* is translated "idle" from *Strong's Concordance* #692, and means unprofitable; useless; barren; slow. We will give an account for our idle, unprofitable, useless, barren words. Have you ever said, "Well, I'm just afraid to go to church today. I know Pastor is going to say something awful about me."

"Yep, he did. He said I had an Unloving spirit in me. I knew he was going to say something bad about me. See, I have been trying to get myself all built up and be a good man of God, but he just told me I did not like myself." Well, you are going to get what you said and believed.

If we do not recognize the problem, we cannot be healed. I said to a pastor the other day, "You just don't like yourself, do you? Well, do you or don't you?"

"No, Pastor, I don't like myself. I have struggled with this for years."

I said, "Thank God."

He said, "Thank God?"

I said, "Yeah, now we can deal with it. You have been trapped and you have been tormented for years. God does not want you to bless people when you yourself are not blessed." Amen?

Are you the best thing since peanut butter? Sure. By your words you are justified or condemned, so you need to watch what you say. Matthew 12:37

It is not just what you *say*. It comes from the abundance of the *heart*. Speaking is only part of your spiritual dynamics, what we see on the *outside*. When you are thinking fearful thoughts on the *inside*, guess what you are going to be doing or saying pretty soon. It has to manifest! I want you to understand that every thought you have, whether it lines up with God or not, must manifest in your life either by deed or by speech.

Proverbs 26:2 says, "The curse causeless shall not come," but if you listen to those words of Fear, guess what is going to manifest. Fear will surely come. If you have Fear, and you take that into Rejection and an Unloving spirit, then the words that Fear and Rejection say will demand fulfillment in your life.

That entire verse reads, "As the bird by wandering, as the swallow by flying, so the curse causeless shall not come." Those words are looking for a place to land.

If you listen to the words that people say against you or take in their actions against you and you take that into your heart and believe it, the fruit of it is right there. It begins within you and it shall manifest. You allowed it to take root within you, instead of taking it captive.

The evil one came to Jesus and found nothing in Him.

> **Hereafter I will not talk much with you: for the prince of this world cometh, and hath nothing in me.** John 14:30

If that person says something to you and his words develop a thought within you, that thought was already within you. It has just linked to the words of the other person. If the high octane ping on the inside of you does not go away, then you have those thoughts of Fear or Rejection about yourself.

"I just know I am the worst thing ever."

That feeling is the fruit of those words and you have become one with them. You have come into agreement with them and your faith in those words has brought forth fruit in your life. You have made the word of that person the new word of God for your life. And you have made the Word of God just the opposite: evil for your life.

If you repent and pull the words down, but you cannot get rid of them, then you need deliverance and ministry. They need to go!

So let's summarize what you can do with all of this knowledge to fight Fear in your life. You now take what you know and exercise it through wisdom. There are three dimensions of being free.

1. Know the truth, because the truth shall make you free. John 8:32
2. Resist the devil. James 4:7
3. Cast the devil out by having someone minister to you according to 1 Corinthians 12.

TEMPTATION

There are two dimensions of thought where sin is concerned. First there is temptation and then there is the reality of evil or sin that is already living within you.

The devil will tempt you through your thoughts

Your enemy has the ability to speak to your mind, to your spirit. He is a spirit. When Satan walked up and down through the earth, he was walking in the dimension of the spirituality of man.

Evil spirits have access to your spirit. They are spirit. They speak and then you develop a consciousness, because you are in contact with your heart intellectually. You think on two dimensions: in your spirit man and in your soulish man. Your thoughts can become one for God, or they can become one for evil.

Hebrews says the Word of God is a discerner of the thoughts and intents of the heart and is able to separate the soul from the spirit.

> **For the word of God *is* quick, and powerful, and sharper than any twoedged sword, piercing even to the dividing asunder of soul and spirit, and of the joints and marrow, and *is* a discerner of the thoughts and intents of the heart.**
>
> Hebrews 4:12

So the Word of God gives us a new way of thinking spiritually. Eventually our mind is renewed by the washing of the water of the Word. Then we become one with the mind of Christ, which is the Word of God: what God thinks and what He says.

Here you become one in your thinking. Every thought that comes in your heart and soul that does not match the way God thinks must be cast down. You catch it, you hold it, you look at it, and you say, "Match up."

Now temptation can come to you and seem just as real as if an evil spirit itself were present. You have to understand the thoughts you have may not be from the sin living within. The tempter may be coming to try to get a foothold in your life. You have to really pay attention.

Seven Steps to Sin is available through our bookstore to help you discern whether or not the sin is living within you or if it is just temptation. You may have become one with sin, or you just had a thought and did not realize it was only temptation. Don't assume you were participating just because you had the thought.

Temptation at all levels is not sin because the Bible says Jesus was tempted in all points such as we are, yet was without sin. Hebrews 4:15 Temptation can bring with it every feeling and every thought as if *you were evil itself.* You do not have to follow every thought or feeling or emotion that comes to you and, even if you have something within you, you do not have to let it manifest.

You grab it by its scrawny neck, drag it screaming into the light and say, "Pastor, look what I found in me! I found this creature in me just squawking and carrying on. I got it! I see it! I want it gone!" Boy, is that spirit in trouble then! Time to ring its neck!

The two dimensions of sin are temptation and then the actuality of sin becoming part of you. Jesus said sin is in the *heart.* Mark 7:15 Paul said sin is *within.* Romans 7:15 He did not say it *was him;* he said it was something *within* him that made him do evil.

Paul did not say it was him; he said it was something within him that made him do evil. It was sin that dwelt within. You must be acutely aware of temptation and do not always think it is sin. You will know it is sin if it becomes part of you. You will start acting it out.

If you have a thought of Bitterness, it could just be temptation. The devil could be saying something against your neighbor, accusing your brother to you. That is temptation. If you allow it to come into your heart and you start to meditate on it and rise up and tell your brother, "I hate you," it is no longer temptation at that point. That is sin manifesting through you. You need to repent and get rid of it. This is basic spiritual discernment, basic spiritual life.

An evil spirit can speak through you, or it can be you yourself speaking through your memes. It can be one or the other. So how do you know the difference? A sudden short-term reality could just be you falling into temptation.

Recognize it and repent for it. Then you have taken every thought captive. You realize it was either something within you or it was a temptation and you deal with it. That is the process of being free. The more you fall and the more you repent and recognize it, the stronger you become. That is how you stand against temptation.

A long-term manifestation would be when a spirit is speaking through you. If you see something long-term, you no longer have temptation; you have a spirit involved.

If you cannot resist what you have been convicted of, that is good evidence a spirit is involved. For example, if someone who gets delivered of adultery or pornography walks into an office and sees a centerfold magazine, what does he do with that? Temptation is still there, but he's convicted.

In the moment of conviction, he takes the book and sticks it in his pocket, planning to get rid of it, but he continues to meditate.

That opens the door for that spirit to come back in, or maybe it never left. Now how do we know the difference? We would know it if he fell and went back into pornography as a lifestyle. That is an indication a spirit is involved.

Let me say something to you, because you need to understand this. You can fall into temptation and it doesn't mean an evil spirit has come to be with you. It just means you yielded to it. You need to be quick to recognize, quick to repent and quick to resist. That is exactly how you take authority over it.

You could have a spirit of Occultism tempting you. If you have a drawing towards spiritualism, the paranormal or anything that programs you to believe the 2nd heaven would be right for you, that is a serious situation.

When you have a desire to watch something and cannot stop it, the spirit of Occultism could be tempting you into that realm. And it is still temptation until you agree with it and become one with it, taking it as your own thought.

Don't forget you can easily be tempted by something from which you already have been delivered. Remember, when the evil spirit is cast out, it wanders through a dry place looking for a place of rest and finding none, comes back to its original house. The house is either filled or empty. Matthew 12:43-44 So there is always temptation to go back.

OCCULTISM

Anything that involves esoteric knowledge and the invisible world, like magic, can attract you because God has created you to have contact with Him spiritually and the devil knows it. Long-term drawing towards the invisible spirit world and things like Star Trek can draw you into Occultism.

Some of the fruits of this occultic spirit include the paranormal. You can have power. You can do magical things. You can bend a spoon. You can levitate. You can be transformed. You can believe there is life on other planets.

We are being programmed by paranormal shows on TV and that is why people go to psychics. In the *Ladies Home Journal* there was an article on psychics and the people who are using them. People are spending over 100 million dollars a year just on psychic hotlines in America alone.

Ninety percent of those using psychics are females between the ages of 30 and 45 who want a change in life. They are reaching out for knowledge and information. That creates the desire for the paranormal, but they are tapping into knowledge that did not come from God. They are tapping into the devil's design for them.

The devil can bless you. Do not think that the devil comes just as an agent of destruction; he also comes as an angel of light. There is no such thing as white magic and black magic, because it is all evil. A white lie and a black lie are equal.

A List of Fears

What is the fruit of Fear? It is all the diseases in the soul or the body that are the result of what Fear is doing to you spiritually. The teaching on *Fear, Stress and Physiology* gives you the complete physiological and soulish long-term consequences such as heart conditions, mitral valve prolapse, irritable bowel syndrome, malabsorption, asthma, and reflux.

AGORAPHOBIA

Agoraphobia is Fear that locks you away in your house forever. That is bondage. It will keep you from enjoying life and keep you avoiding everything in life.

BIGOTRY

Bigotry is not only for races, but how about churches? Denominationalism comes out of Fear. Racism comes out of Fear and includes the Fear of other races and Fear of other people.

BITTERNESS

Bitterness is a big deal because it fills you with Distrust. Bitterness fills you with Fear of man, Fear of Rejection and Fear of Failure.

CHURCH MEMBERS HAVING FEAR

Let's see what Isaiah says about this.

> **13Hear, ye *that are* far off, what I have done; and, ye *that are* near, acknowledge my might.**
>
> **14The sinners in Zion are afraid; fearfulness hath surprised the hypocrites. Who among us shall dwell with the devouring fire? who among us shall dwell with everlasting burnings?**
>
> **15He that walketh righteously, and speaketh uprightly; he that despiseth the gain of oppressions, that shaketh his hands from holding of bribes, that stoppeth his ears from hearing of blood, and shutteth his eyes from seeing evil;**
>
> Isaiah 33:13-15

"The sinners in Zion are afraid." Zion stands for the church. "Fearfulness has surprised the hypocrites. Who among us shall dwell with the devouring fire?" That means who among us can stand before the living God, who is the devouring fire?

Who among us shall dwell with everlasting burnings and be able to stand in the judgment of God? He that walketh righteously."

What are the characteristics of being free of Fear?

- Walking righteously
- Speaking uprightly (Watch your mouth.)
- Despising the gain of oppression
- Shaking your hands from holding a bribe
- Stopping your ears from the hearing of blood
- Shutting your eyes from seeing evil

These murder flicks and horror stories are opening your heart and your eyes to evil. Your protection is to shut your eyes from seeing evil and to stop your ears from the hearing of blood. If you have blown it here, do not go into Guilt and Fear, but come into conviction. Get before God, repent and ask Him to deliver you.

Make up your mind that you are not going to be curious about evil any more. If you are curious about evil, you have an evil spirit within you which produces evil thoughts. It draws you to the bizarre, to see someone being mutilated. It is the desire to see, and to see, and to see.

That drawing is not part of you. That drawing comes from an evil spirit that needs to be fulfilled. He wants to become one with you and make you one with him, so he can terrify you. He wants to torment you; he wants to torment your children with Fear of the very same thing in their lives.

You can also have bad dreams and nightmares coming out of phobic projection. It comes whether you have watched horror films or not because it does not necessarily need a medium to come in; it is just there.

You need to get a reality check. This is not fun and games; this is a real battle for your life. I do not mean to scare you, but I think there *is* a type of fear that needs to be instilled within you and that is respect for the living God.

You are begging God to heal you. Do you want God to help you? There are some things you are going to have to do for yourself before He will.

Do you think God is going to deliver you from Fear when you keep reprogramming yourself with the very same thing? Of course He isn't, because you are giving place to the devil. Get away from that stuff!

> **Let no corrupt communication proceed out of your mouth, but that which is good to the use of edifying, that it may minister grace unto the hearers.** Ephesians 4:29

Newspapers are detrimental to your health. All you see in them is who has been killed, murdered, shot, robbed, or died and is listed in the obituary column. Many newspapers do not even print birth announcements anymore. You need to guard your heart.

If you are drawn to the eleven o'clock news to see what went wrong in the world, you have a problem. If you are observing world affairs objectively, then it will not bother you. You have to know what your spirit is made of. I observe mankind from my heavenly place with Christ Jesus and God, looking down.

If you are drawn to that stuff and you already have Fear in that area, then you are reinforcing it. If you withdraw from it in Fear, which is worse? You need some balance.

Don't withdraw from it in Fear. Look at it according to knowledge. This is time for you to go into discernment. You say, "I have a Fear of evil and when I see that stuff it just feeds it." Yes and then it torments you. Now is not the time to go into Fear. Now is the time to recognize that you have a spiritual problem.

I can be exposed to things that go wrong and it is a shocker to the senses, but at the same time I do not have to make it part of my life. Because someone had a wreck today does not mean I am not going to drive. Because someone had her purse snatched does not mean my wife is going to lose hers.

Are you taught to be afraid, or are you taught to have wisdom according to knowledge? Would you like to replace Fear with knowledge and wisdom? You can live your life with wisdom and not be afraid.

Even though you have knowledge and wisdom about a potential problem, you still can have an acceleration of fight or flight because that is the way you are designed. You do not have to stay in that though, because you are a spiritual person and you understand. If something becomes a phobia to you, then you are tormented and ruled and controlled. You have an evil spirit.

When you go into a parking lot at night, do you take precautions? Yes. Do you lock your door? Yes. Do you park in a lighted area? Yes. Do you look around to make sure there is no one around? Yes. But do you do it in Fear? No.

As parents, we can instill Fear as a method of teaching. Instead, teach your children knowledge about the problem. Limit the risks by giving them wisdom concerning what action to take.

Do not try to control your children through Fear. Teach them so they can make a decision based not in Fear, but according to knowledge. There is a difference.

Did your mama and daddy teach you with wisdom and knowledge? Or did they just try to control you, putting Fear of a given situation in you? They actually opened the door to spirits of Fear and then called that wisdom and knowledge! There is a distinct difference.

You cannot let Fear rule you. Fear is like a dog who knows whether you are afraid of it or not. If you have confidence, that dog will back away from you, but if you show any amount of Fear, it feeds on your Fear.

In these scriptures, keeping your eyes from seeing evil and your ears from the shedding of blood is connected with what? It says the sinners are afraid and the hypocrites are fearful.

So if you do not apply these scriptures to your life and make them part of your spiritual mentality, what's going to come? Fear and fearfulness. It's right here in the Word! Fear and fearfulness are going to come to you, even if you are a faithful church member.

Gaining Freedom

So how would you begin to get rid of your Fear and your fearfulness? Start applying these principles. If you would make this adjustment, if you would take the time before God to repent, you would be surprised how fast God would meet you.

Deliverance does not have to be like an old-fashioned horse doctor yanking teeth out of a horse. It can come quickly as a work of the Spirit. You can be set free just like that. You need to be prepared for that to happen.

The first element of freedom is to know the truth, and the truth shall make you free, because you have new memes that have surpassed the old ones. John 8:31-32 Now you are following the mind of Christ, the Word of God, which is washing your mind.

You are following a new way of thinking. The old one is still there, but who are you listening to, the voice of the devil or the voice of the Good Shepherd?

Isaiah says the man or woman who follows the voice of the Good Shepherd will be a in a good place!

> **He shall dwell on high: his place of defence *shall be* the munitions of rocks: bread shall be given him; his waters *shall be* sure.** Isaiah 33:16

Wow! There is a provision for safety. You can be safe and *still* have Fear all around you.

How many things were you afraid of in your life that never came to pass? How much time have you wasted in projection, avoidance and displacement around those issues? How much sleep have you lost?

Did your fears ever come to pass? No.

What you Fear can come to pass, but Fear can be just plain torment that something will come to pass. First John 4:18 part three says, "Fear hath torment." Torment is an open door for all of your nightmares and day-mares.

DISTRUST

Distrust and Suspicion are big problems. Both are a form of Fear.

ENVY AND JEALOUSY

Envy and Jealousy is also rooted in Fear, even though Envy and Jealousy can be separate. Envy and Jealousy can come out of the Fear of competition.

EXCESSIVE TALKATIVENESS

Excessive talkativeness is a tremendous fruit of anxiety and Fear.

FEAR OF ABANDONMENT

Fear of Abandonment is when you feel like you are going to be abandoned by God and others. The first thing you have to do is to settle the matter: you are not abandoned by God. You are accepted by God.

FEAR OF ANIMALS

Fear of animals like dogs or cats is a big one. Let's also include bugs, spiders, chiggers, dinosaurs, parasites, etc. We could call it Fear of creatures. I promise you, when I see a black widow spider or a snake I am going to back off. It won't be in Fear, but is my heart racing a little bit? Yes.

Fight or flight is a natural part of your creation. A racing heart, respiratory rate increase, adrenaline rush—all of that is how God created you to respond. But that is not the same as long-term phobic realities. Fight or flight is designed to be situational, but when the situation is continually projected into the future you have a spirit of Fear.

I was bitten by a dog when I was four years old. It was a white dog. My eye popped out of the socket and it was just dangling. They put my eye back in. Am I afraid of dogs? No, I am not, but I was told the story all my life to reinforce the Fear. I do not have any Fear of animals, including dogs. Do I have a respect for them? Yes. Do I have wisdom concerning them? Yes.

Teach your children not to be afraid of snakes, not to be afraid of spiders. We teach the difference between good snakes and poisonous snakes, good spiders and bad spiders. We teach that spiders in general are good, snakes in general are good, but we must understand creation. We do not teach from Fear but from knowledge and wisdom.

FEAR OF ANOTHER'S BITTERNESS

Fear of another person's anger is like Fear of Retaliation; it is still Fear of man. There is Fear of Violence. Remember that you have seven spirits (or armour) that answer to Bitterness that could be against other people. You also can have the same seven realities against yourself and be afraid of experiencing those same seven realities from others.

Bitterness is a principality with seven evil spirits answering to it, each much worse than the former. These are Unforgiveness, Resentment, Retaliation, Anger and Wrath, Hatred, Violence and Murder.

When you are dealing with Bitterness, all of these are progressively worse than the former, producing a final fruit of Murder, including Murder with the tongue. That is the fruit of Bitterness.

There are three dimensions of the fruit of Bitterness. First, you may have these realities in yourself against another person. Second, you may have all of these components against yourself. These are Self-Unforgiveness, Self-Resentment, Self-Retaliation, Self-Anger, Self-Hatred, Self-Violence (which is Self-Abuse) and Self-Murder (which is Suicide, coming out of Self-Hatred and Self-Bitterness).

Third, you may be afraid of all of these realities from others against yourself. We have Fear of another's Bitterness. Not only do we project Bitterness against others, not only do we project Bitterness against ourselves, but we are afraid of Bitterness from others, which is Fear of man. That also includes Fear of Rejection and Fear of Failure.

Do not be afraid of their faces
Do not be afraid of their words

Be not afraid of their faces: for I *am* with thee to deliver thee, saith the LORD. Jeremiah 1:8

The LORD *is* on my side; I will not fear: what can man do unto me? Psalm 118:6

There is negative Fear of God, when we project that God is bitter toward us. You can project that God is going to get even with you and that God has not forgiven you. The

Word says He forgives you, but you do not believe it. You believe that He forgives someone else, but He has not forgiven you. Well, have you ever heard that the Accuser of the brethren is cast down and he accused the brethren before God day and night?

> **And I heard a loud voice saying in heaven, Now is come salvation, and strength, and the kingdom of our God, and the power of his Christ: for the accuser of our brethren is cast down, which accused them before our God day and night.** Revelation 12:10

When people think God is mad at them, they are listening to an Accusing spirit.

FEAR OF ANOTHER'S WORDS

The Bible says, "Fear not what man can do unto you." Remember the old saying, "Sticks and stones may break my bones, but words will never hurt me." That is an absolute lie. Words hurt. You could have Fear of verbal abuse. You could also be afraid of a person's words, even though their words were not abusive at all. There could be Fear of conflict.

FEAR OF AUTHORITY

Fear of authority brings Fear of judgment and Fear of punishment. There are three major Fears that feed Fear of Authority: Fear of man, Fear of rejection and Fear of failure. Fear of abandonment really can be included too.

FEAR OF BEING ALONE

It is amazing that we are afraid of people, yet we still need them. That is just Fear of man. Fear of being with others comes out of Fear of Rejection, Fear of man, Fear of Failure, Fear of Abandonment, Fear of being alone.

FEAR OF BEING FREE

You choose to believe God when Fear comes and it is raging in your head. If you want to be free, but are afraid to be free, you are never going to be free. That would be Fear of being free.

I have had many people come to me and say, "I don't know who I'm going to be when I'm delivered. I'm afraid of who I will be." That is Fear of being free.

There are people who want to stay in bondage. That is their prison. They have been in there almost 20 years and when you let them out on the street, why do they want to go back? The prison is a safe place for them. They have Fear of being free.

FEAR OF CHANGE

Fear of change represents the unknown.

FEAR OF CLOSED PLACES

Claustrophobia is a spirit: the Fear of closed places.

FEAR OF COMMITMENT

Fear of commitment is also Fear of responsibility.

FEAR OF DARKNESS

In the Song of Solomon, there is Fear of darkness.

> **They all hold swords, *being* expert in war: every man *hath* his sword upon his thigh because of fear in the night.**
> Song of Solomon 3:8

FEAR OF DEATH

You may have Fear of Death and Fear of losing life, which concerns the length of our years. You may be thinking, "Pastor, if you do not stop it, you are going to take away everything that is important to me. I have a right to be concerned about death."

If you have a right to be concerned about death, do you have a right to be concerned about life after death? My faith is not in what death can or cannot do to me. My faith is in life after death.

The Bible says that in that day, at the end of the millennium, all the enemies of Christ shall be defeated, the last of which shall be Death. Even if you died in your generation, when the last trump sounds you shall be raised from the dead. 1 Corinthians 15:22

There are two dimensions to death—one is of God and one is of the devil. There is a death that the devil uses, and then there is the allotted time of life in which God takes us. There is a difference.

Death is not necessarily evil, but it is evil when disease takes us. I do not believe God's will planned that we should die in the pain of disease as a method of ending our 70 to 80 years in the promised land. The enemies of Christ shall be defeated, the last of which is Death. There is a spirit of Death at work to kill people. I consider that to be a principality called the Angel of Death.

When we are resurrected from the dead, we shall be like Him and we shall have a glorified body. After He was raised from the dead, Jesus was able to eat food. He could appear in a room and never walk through the door because He was not bound by the material, molecular composition of matter. He showed us the glorified body and its ability to operate from the dimensions of spirit in the physical world and the spiritual world.

Having a glorified body is part of our destiny. This means in that day, after the resurrection when we come back as kings with Christ in the millennium, we will be able to operate in the physical dimension and in the spiritual dimension. We will be able to see the invisible evil spirits that are trying to plague natural man in the millennium. The spirit of Death will be defeated.

The book of Hebrews says,

> **And deliver them who through fear of death were all their lifetime subject to bondage.** Hebrews 2:15

Disease produces Fear of dying and Fear of Death. We can fear Death in many ways. Fear of disease is why insurance companies and the medical profession—especially the pharmaceutical industry—are making a fortune off your fears.

Fear of disease. Fear of accidents. Fear of injury. Fear of assault. You do not live in Fear. You are to live with wisdom. It is possible for you to have wisdom about potential problems in the future and not be in Fear concerning them. You could become so phobic projecting the possibilities that a spirit of Fear could take you over into a phobic reality.

You can make provision for evil, but do not go into Fear concerning it because it may never happen. For example, if you live in an area where crime is prevalent, you might install an alarm system in your house. You would be doing that out of wisdom, not out of Fear.

Fear can set you up. A very real, invisible kingdom communicates just as easily in the spirit when you send an e-mail across America through electronic devices. There is no distance in the spirit. That kingdom is a very intelligent kingdom. It knows what it is doing to mankind.

FEAR OF DELIVERANCE

Fear of deliverance would be when you are afraid to be ministered to and afraid of an evil spirit manifesting in your life.

FEAR OF DISAPPROVAL

In the call of Ezekiel, God told him not to be afraid of their faces. What about when Jeremiah was called?

Jeremiah says,

> **4Then the word of the LORD came unto me, saying,**
>
> **5Before I formed thee in the belly I knew thee; and before thou camest forth out of the womb I sanctified thee, and I ordained thee a prophet unto the nations.**
>
> **6Then said I, Ah, Lord God! behold, I cannot speak: for I am a child.**
>
> **7But the Lord said unto me, Say not, I am a child: for thou shalt go to all that I shall send thee, and whatsoever I command thee thou shalt speak.**
>
> **8Be not afraid of their faces: for I *am* with thee to deliver thee, saith the LORD.** Jeremiah 1:4-8

"Be not afraid of their faces..." There is Fear of facial expressions. Have you ever thought that others disagreed with you? Did they show it? Did that intimidate you? When you became intimidated, Fear of man was intimidating you. How about Fear of disapproval, which is also rooted in Fear of Rejection?

FEAR OF ENEMIES

How about Fear of enemies? Fear of man is similar, but Fear of an enemy is a different story. Have you ever had a bill collector call you on the phone? Is that a friend or an enemy?

God will give you wisdom in making peace with your enemies. Owing someone money could make that person your enemy. The Bible says the person to whom you owe money has become your master and you have become his slave. An enemy could be anyone.

It says in the Psalms,

> **The LORD *is* on my side; I will not fear: what can man do unto me?** Psalm 118:6

The book of Proverbs says,

> **26I also will laugh at your calamity; I will mock when your fear cometh;**
>
> **27When your fear cometh as desolation, and your destruction cometh as a whirlwind; when distress and anguish cometh upon you.**
>
> **28Then shall they call upon me, but I will not answer; they shall seek me early, but they shall not find me:**
>
> **29For that they hated knowledge, and did not choose the fear of the LORD:**
>
> **30They would none of my counsel: they despised all my reproof.**

> **[31]Therefore shall they eat of the fruit of their own way, and be filled with their own devices.** Proverbs 1:26-31

Now this is a very tough scripture because this is where God does not answer prayer.

FEAR OF FAILURE

Fear of Failure does not allow you to be wrong. Do you know what the Word says?

> **For a just *man* falleth seven times, and riseth up again: but the wicked shall fall into mischief.** Proverbs 24:16

God has made provision for you to fail, so why should you have Fear of Failure? If someone is holding you to that degree of responsibility, plead failure. Say, "I am but dust and I reserve the right to fail. I take responsibility to make a change in the failure."

If you take this position in your thinking when people reject you and you have failed, how will they respond? They can say nothing because they themselves fail. Perfectionism is a form of Fear and will not allow for failure. It says this, "Unless I have my hands on everything and am moving all the pieces at the same time, this will not work out."

You must make provision for failure, because God made provision for it. Though a just man falls seven times, he rises up again. Proverbs 24:16

> **Many *are* the afflictions of the righteous: but the LORD delivereth him out of them all.** Psalm 34:19

Perfectionism is rooted in Fear and it involves two dimensions: knowledge and movement. Perfectionism and Control are slightly related in that there is a spirit of Fear behind them both saying, "My future is in my own hands. I must have all knowledge about all things, so I can move all the pieces around under my eyesight and my 'mind-sight,' because my destiny is my own."

Perfectionism has caused more spirits of Fear to enter into children than you can imagine. Our society is based on success, but God's society is based on success that begins in failure. Man's society makes no allowance for failure, but God says, "In your weakness, I am made strong."

> **9 And he said unto me, My grace is sufficient for thee: for my strength is made perfect in weakness. Most gladly therefore will I rather glory in my infirmities, that the power of Christ may rest upon me.**
>
> **10 Therefore I take pleasure in infirmities, in reproaches, in necessities, in persecutions, in distresses for Christ's sake: for when I am weak, then am I strong.** 2 Corinthians 12:9-10

Man's society says we have no place for the weak, so let's create abortion and euthanasia. Let's create a society in which the disabled or weak ones are eliminated. In fact, let's go a little step further. Let's do some genetic testing in utero.

If we find we are going to have a disabled child, or the child will develop a particular disabling disease in his/her lifetime, then let's abort now and try again. It is an attempt to bypass the penalty of the curse, out of Fear.

There is great scriptural evidence of God making provision for the disabled one. Jonathan's son Mephibosheth was crippled and David took him in as a son. The Word of God has always made provision for the disabled and the disadvantaged.

This is not a society of the strong. This is a society that has been sold to sin and needs deliverance, freedom and salvation. So you must make allowance for weakness.

Fear will not let you make allowance for weakness. Are you always striving with yourself? When you see your weaknesses, do you go directly into Fear, Unbelief and Doubt and Self-Hatred, because Fear has told you that your value is based on success?

Your value has nothing to do with success. Your value is based on the fact that God created you from the foundation of the world. Even if your mother conceived you in sin, Psalm 139 says you are here by God's permission and ordination. By the way, you are going to get a new body anyway, so what's the problem?

Consider the parable of the talents. What if I blow it? This is not a statement of faith; it is a statement of Fear. A lord came and gave one servant one talent, another five talents and the last ten talents. When he came back later, the one that had been given ten talents made ten more. The one that had been given five, made five more.

The servant who had been given one said, "I am afraid of you, Master, because you are a very stern and very solemn master. I was afraid that I would lose it. So when you came back, I would not have one talent I went and hid it in the dirt because of my Fear of you. Here, lord, is your talent back."

His lord was wroth with him and said, "Thou unfaithful servant. The least you could have done is to have taken the talent down to the bank, put it in the money market or a CD and given me back a small interest. But you hid it in Fear of me."

That servant had Fear of Failure. The lord was wroth with the servant, not because he gave the talent back to him or because he did not make any interest on the money, but because he had Fear of Failure.

FEAR OF BEING CONTROLLED

Domination is Fear of being controlled. Nations declare war on each other because of Fear, or Lust, or a need for power. Hitler had it made. For much of his administration, he had become known as a wonderful ruler by his people and by the world. But Hitler had a spiritual defect in that he was controlled by Paranoia. He had to guarantee his own safety, even in his success.

In his Paranoia, he attacked the nations around him to extend borders of protection so he would not have to deal with anyone's interference. He was guaranteeing his own success, but he ruled in Paranoia, which, in turn, produced dementia in him. He became insane.

The books are saying he was not insane, he was just a genius. But extreme genius is a form of insanity. Most people who are extreme geniuses never serve God and most die at an early age. When you look up the word "genius" in the dictionary, it means guardian spirit.

According to ancient Roman belief, a guardian spirit—a tutelary deity—is assigned to a person at birth. It is supposed to influence one's destiny. Webster's defines "genies" as a sort of imaginary intermediate beings who are between men and angels. Some are good and some are bad.

Do you think evil spirits have intellect? Do you think evil spirits are able to be composers and writers and inventors? These evil spirits have been around for six thousand years. They were around before Adam.

I think we need a reality check. That is why churches today need to teach spiritual dynamics from a proper perspective. I'm not talking only about the casting out of evil spirits, but we need to teach understanding of the 2nd heaven ruled by Satan.

You need to really think about what is happening here on this planet. Carl Jung was considered to be a genius, but his "genius," according to his own words, came to him from a spirit guide named Philemon. He said Philemon taught him everything he knew through visions and automatic handwriting.

The Bible says holy men of old wrote as they were moved by the Holy Spirit. 2 Peter 1:21 Many people write under the inspiration of the Holy Spirit. However, automatic handwriting is occultic.

Carl Jung's genius for modern day psychology came from an evil spirit. So much for genius! The genius behind Carl Jung was supposed to help mankind. But modern-day psychotherapy is literally based on necromancy, which is contact with the dead.

Where do you think the mentality for Hitler's Aryan race of supremacy came from? It came from the evil spirit Genius. At first it came masquerading as good, but behind it was destruction.

FEAR OF FAMILIES

I want to help you deal with your mother and father and brother and sister and others in your families. I want to help you deal with the people whom you fear the most. Matriarchal control and patriarchal control are very big problems in America today and in the world. You are an adult. Your parents do not have the right to tell you one thing to do. When they try to, tell them that you are an adult.

If you would take that stand in love, you would have control of your life and Fear would not rule you in that dimension. Do you think you can do that and still honor your mother and father? It has not happened yet because you are afraid of them.

FEAR OF GAINING WEIGHT

Fear of gaining weight is rooted in the Unloving spirit and weight gain comes from the lack of serotonin. When you have a spiritual problem involving Self-Rejection, Self-Bitterness and Guilt, the pineal gland causes serotonin to be under-produced.

You already did not feel good about yourself, but now you have a lowered production of serotonin. You feel even worse about yourself and then you want to go eat, but you have a Fear of eating because you know you will gain weight. So there is Fear of gaining weight.

FEAR OF GHOSTS AND SPIRITS

Matthew says,

> **And when the disciples saw him walking on the sea, they were troubled, saying, It is a spirit; and they cried out for fear.** Matthew 14:26

They cried for Fear when Jesus came walking on the water. When they saw Him they said, "It is a ghost!" They became afraid. They were afraid of Casper. Well, Casper is supposed to be the friendly ghost, isn't he? But it was not Casper, it was Jesus. What a surprise!

Timothy says,

> **For God hath not given us the spirit of fear; but of power, and of love, and of a sound mind.** 2 Timothy 1:7

FEAR OF GIVING AND RECEIVING LOVE

An element of Fear is found in 1 John 4:18, part four. "He that feareth is not made perfect in love." That means you are not able to give and receive love without Fear.

FEAR OF HUMILIATION

There is also Fear of humiliation. I was talking to someone and said, "Very honestly, I reserve the right to be wrong. I have had to change my mind many times. I reserve the right to be wrong, but I also reserve the right to make the corrections when I am wrong. I don't have all the answers. And besides, all of us find ourselves in ignorance many times. Do you realize that from a philosophical standpoint, ignorance is a form of knowledge?"

The Bible says, "We see through a glass darkly." 1 Corinthians 13:12 We do not see things the way they really are, so we have to begin to look for it. Philosophically, it goes like this—when you think you have found truth, it is time to begin looking for it. When you think you have an insight, it is time to begin to study and prove it. Reserve the right to be wrong.

FEAR OF INDEPENDENCE

Fear of independence and Fear of being free. One of the things I have noticed in ministry to those with Environmental

Illness is that the disease has made them so dependent, they do not want to be independent. They want to be cared for.

FEAR OF INSANITY

Fear of Insanity is a big one because it has such a stigma.

FEAR OF LOSING YOUR CONFIDENCE

I learned something about Nebuchadnezzar from the book of Daniel that I have never forgotten: God is in control. Even though your enemies rise against you—if you will stay out of Fear, stay in love and keep yourself right before God—then God will become your defender.

I learned from Nebuchadnezzar that God raises people up and He sets them down. If God is your Defender, you are going to proceed regardless of your enemy. If you listen to your enemy, you are going to go into defensive maneuvers, which many times are built out of Fear.

If people speak evil against you, maybe they have seen a defect in you and are telling the truth. They are taking advantage of it and using it against you, but maybe it is time to listen. There is nothing wrong with constructive criticism, and even "destructive" criticism can have an element of truth.

Now slanderers and liars never tell the truth, but the devil is always looking for a crack in your armor. Sometimes he will use other people to tell you about it. When that happens do you lose your confidence? Do you go into Fear? No. You go before God and get that repaired. Let the Potter remold you. Do that in faith, not in Fear.

When you see the defect in your life, do not withdraw. Don't lose your confidence. Run right into the fire and say, "Mold me and make me, God. Take this defect!"

The Potter will keep breaking your vessel and reworking it until it becomes a vessel of honor. Don't run from your cracks and your defects. Run to God *with* them and say, "Father, pour on the fire." That is the baptism of fire John the Baptist talked about.

He said,

> **...he shall baptize you with the Holy Ghost, and *with* fire:**
> Matthew 3:11

This baptism of fire is the sanctifying work of the Holy Spirit to purge us from dross and impurities—to make us into a vessel of honor and pure gold. So don't withdraw in your defects, but run to God with them. If someone comes up and points out a defect say, "Thank you."

What if it is not true? Say thank you anyway. You do not want to get into a verbal battle, because you will be in the flesh.

FEAR OF LOSING YOUR SALVATION

Fear of losing your salvation is Accusation against God.

FEAR OF LOSS OF RELATIONSHIP

Many people have a hard time accepting constructive criticism because of Rejection. Do you know how hard it is for me as a pastor, even with members of my staff, to tell them the truth? Sometimes I just withdraw and tell God, "Please, talk to them."

When God does not, I have to go to them and say, "I sure love you, but we have to talk about this." Am I in Fear? Probably, for the moment, because I do not want to lose the relationship. That would be Fear of the loss of relationship.

But what does the Bible say about that? "An open rebuke is better than secret love." Proverbs 27:5 So if I love you, I am going to tell you the truth.

FEAR OF MAN

Fear of man is a big deal. Some of the first scriptures about Fear of man and Fear of God were found when Adam and Eve hid in the garden.

Genesis says,

> **And they heard the voice of the LORD God walking in the garden in the cool of the day: and Adam and his wife hid themselves from the presence of the LORD God amongst the trees of the garden.** Genesis 3:8

They had Fear of God, but it is the same thing that produces Fear of man. God came down and walked with them in the cool of the day just as if He were a man. When they heard Him coming as was His custom, they ran and hid out of Fear. But the Bible says not to fear man.

> **16Behold, I send you forth as sheep in the midst of wolves: be ye therefore wise as serpents, and harmless as doves.**
>
> **17But beware of men: for they will deliver you up to the councils, and they will scourge you in their synagogues;**

There you have opposition from religious leaders.

> **18And ye shall be brought before governors and kings for my sake, for a testimony against them and the Gentiles.**

Now you have opposition from political leaders.

> **19But when they deliver you up, take no thought how or what ye shall speak: for it shall be given you in that same hour what ye shall speak.**
>
> **20For it is not ye that speak, but the Spirit of your Father which speaketh in you.**
>
> **21And the brother shall deliver up the brother to death, and the father the child: and the children shall rise up against *their* parents, and cause them to be put to death.**

There is opposition from relatives.

> **22And ye shall be hated of all *men* for my name's sake: but he that endureth to the end shall be saved.**
>
> **23But when they persecute you in this city, flee ye into another: for verily I say unto you, Ye shall not have gone over the cities of Israel, till the Son of man be come.**
>
> Matthew 10:16-23

Here is persecution, enmity or Hatred against you from the world. That means mankind in general. Do not fear man.

> **26Fear them not therefore: for there is nothing covered, that shall not be revealed; and hid, that shall not be known.**
>
> **27What I tell you in darkness, *that* speak ye in light: and what ye hear in the ear, *that* preach ye upon the housetops.**
>
> **28And fear not them which kill the body, but are not able to kill the soul: but rather fear him which is able to destroy both soul and body in hell.**
>
> **29Are not two sparrows sold for a farthing? and one of them shall not fall on the ground without your Father.**
>
> **30But the very hairs of your head are all numbered.**
>
> **31Fear ye not therefore, ye are of more value than many sparrows.** Matthew 10:26-31

So whether you are persecuted by religious leaders, political rulers, relatives, or just general members of mankind, bring this into the context of verse 26. "Fear them not therefore." Do not fear man. Verse 28 says, "Fear not them which kill the body, but are unable to kill the soul: but rather fear Him which is able to destroy both the soul and body in hell."

Verse 29 continues to talk about not fearing, "Are not two sparrows sold for a farthing and not one of them shall fall to the ground without your Father knowing about it?" God the Father recognizes when one bird dies and He takes note of it.

"But the very hairs of your head are numbered. Fear ye not therefore, ye are of more value than many sparrows." Fear not. Fear not man. Fear not the loss of your life.

> **But I will forewarn you whom ye shall fear: Fear him, which after he hath killed hath power to cast into hell; yea, I say unto you, Fear him.** Luke 12:5

> **So that we may boldly say, The Lord *is* my helper, and I will not fear what man shall do unto me.** Hebrews 13:6

Ezekiel says,

> 8**Behold, I have made thy face strong against their faces, and thy forehead strong against their foreheads.**
>
> 9**As an adamant harder than flint have I made thy forehead: fear them not, neither be dismayed at their looks, though they *be* a rebellious house.** Ezekiel 3:8-9

Ezekiel is being encouraged in his mission as a prophet. "Behold I have made thy face strong against their faces and thy forehead strong against their foreheads." This would be Ezekiel's anointing to confront the people in their sins.

"Fear them not, neither be dismayed at their looks." God is telling Ezekiel not to be afraid of the people he would be talking to, nor of someone's facial features.

How often do you scrutinize and try to read people's faces? That is Fear of man, but we are judging each other after the flesh all the time. You do not know the thoughts of a man. The Bible says the only one who knows the thoughts of the man are the man himself and God who made him.

You may make a very big mistake in judging people with this type of discernment, because only God and the person himself know the inner thoughts of that man's heart. He may be acting out a façade, because there may be a defense mechanism operating through him to protect the real thoughts.

If we were to make four biggies out of this, Fear of man is at the top of the list. Next is Fear of Rejection. The third is Fear of Failure. The fourth is Fear of Abandonment. When you think about the Fears in your life, you will find that these four comprise a big part of what you deal with.

Now the rest of the Fears filter in as networking spirits of Fear. When Adam and Eve fell, they were afraid of man. They were afraid of God, and they were ashamed of themselves. An unclean, Unloving spirit came right on in. Fear and uncleanness, or an Unloving spirit, go hand-in-hand. First they felt unclean and then they were afraid.

FEAR OF NATURAL DISASTERS

Do you ever struggle with Fear of natural disasters, earthquakes and the like?

> **1 To the chief Musician for the sons of Korah, A Song upon Alamoth. God *is* our refuge and strength, a very present help in trouble.**
>
> **2 Therefore will not we fear, though the earth be removed, and though the mountains be carried into the midst of the sea;**
>
> **3 *Though* the waters thereof roar *and* be troubled, *though* the mountains shake with the swelling thereof. Selah.**
>
> Psalm 46:1-3

"Though the waters thereof roar and be troubled," means floods, typhoons, and hurricanes. "Though the mountains shake with the swelling thereof," means volcanoes and earthquakes. It says, "We will not fear… Selah." So don't be afraid of what is happening on the earth, "Selah," which means pause and take that in.

One of the signs of the end times is earthquakes in diverse places. Earthquakes are mentioned in 46 books of the Bible. This earth will also be hit twice by asteroids. If you are born again, you will not be here, so don't go into Fear of asteroids. The earth is already in Fear concerning asteroids. They are already making plans to send a rocket up with an atomic bomb on the end of it that will explode and divert what is coming.

They are making these plans now out of Fear. This planet will never be hit by anything of that magnitude until the tribulation period, and then it will be hit twice—once in the sea and once on the land. One third of all of mankind will die.

According to Zechariah, another major earthquake will happen at the end of the tribulation.

> **1Behold, the day of the LORD cometh, and thy spoil shall be divided in the midst of thee.**
>
> **2For I will gather all nations against Jerusalem to battle; and the city shall be taken, and the houses rifled, and the women ravished; and half of the city shall go forth into captivity, and the residue of the people shall not be cut off from the city.**
>
> **3Then shall the LORD go forth, and fight against those nations, as when he fought in the day of battle.**
>
> **4And his feet shall stand in that day upon the mount of Olives, which *is* before Jerusalem on the east, and the mount of Olives shall cleave in the midst thereof toward the east and toward the west, *and there shall be* a very great**

valley; and half of the mountain shall remove toward the north, and half of it toward the south.

5And ye shall flee *to* the valley of the mountains; for the valley of the mountains shall reach unto Azal: yea, ye shall flee, like as ye fled from before the earthquake in the days of Uzziah king of Judah: and the LORD my God shall come, *and* all the saints with thee. Zechariah 14:1-5

It will be in Jerusalem. They have discovered a major earthquake fault right in the middle of Jerusalem. The Bible says Jesus will come back to Jerusalem with the saints to confront the antichrist at Armageddon. The minute His feet hit the Mount of Olives, there will be a massive earthquake.

I like to tell Jewish people, "When the Messiah comes, a major earthquake will happen in Jerusalem. Your prophet Zechariah said that." So anyone who comes and says, "I am Messiah," and the Mount of Olives is still standing intact, he is the false messiah.

If the Jewish people would just go back and read what their own prophets wrote, they would realize that when Messiah comes, the Mount of Olives splits right down the middle. They should not accept any man who comes while the Mount of Olives is still intact, because he is a liar. He is antichrist.

Matthew says,

3And as he sat upon the mount of Olives, the disciples came unto him privately, saying, Tell us, when shall these things be? and what *shall be* the sign of thy coming, and of the end of the world?

4And Jesus answered and said unto them, Take heed that no man deceive you.

5For many shall come in my name, saying, I am Christ; and shall deceive many.

[6]And ye shall hear of wars and rumours of wars: see that ye be not troubled: for all *these things* must come to pass, but the end is not yet.

[7]For nation shall rise against nation, and kingdom against kingdom: and there shall be famines, and pestilences, and earthquakes, in divers places. Matthew 24:3-7

In the world today, at any given time, there are over 40 different wars going on, and it has been this way for generations. "And there shall be famines and pestilences and earthquakes in divers places. And all these are the beginning of sorrows."

The Bible says not to be afraid of natural disasters. Do not be afraid of windstorms. Do not be afraid of tornadoes. Do not be afraid of hurricanes. Do not be afraid of floods. Do not be afraid of earthquakes. Do not be afraid of anything. Take your peace.

What is the worst thing that can happen to you? You can die and go to heaven. So what is your problem?

But at the same time, use wisdom. If there is a location prone to earthquakes, then there is always a risk of an earthquake happening. You have to make a choice. Do you move according to Fear, or according to wisdom, or according to the Lord moving you?

Why are you in a certain place? Because of family, because of your job, because of yourself, or did God send you there? Most people are not where God wants them. Most people are there because of bondage to their mother.

FEAR OF NOT BEING FREE

Fear of *not* being free is thinking you are never going to be free because God is never going to answer your prayers. It is thinking God is never going to deliver you.

FEAR OF NOTHING

Have you ever been afraid, but you did not know what you were afraid of? You are just surrounded by Fear. What torment that is!

> **There were they in great fear, *where* no fear was: for God hath scattered the bones of him that encampeth *against* thee: thou hast put *them* to shame, because God hath despised them.**
> Psalm 53:5

There were they in great Fear, where there was no Fear. Talk about being phobic! They were in great Fear and there was not one reason for them to be afraid. Have you ever found yourself in Fear when there was not one known reason for you to be afraid? You just were afraid.

You could be trembling. You could have heart palpitations. You could have anaphylaxis and throat closure. You could be sweating. You could have rashes and burning skin. You could have cerebral effects, like fuzzy thinking or brain fog.

You could be knock-kneed, trembling and jerking all over the place without one reason for you to be afraid. This is found right in Psalm 53:5. They had Fear when there was nothing to fear. That is Fear of nothing!

You have to realize you've just been "had" by a spirit of Fear that has reinforced itself long-term in your memory through protein synthesis. Unless we have a biologically inherited defect, that is the process.

I find in ministry that most people with fear and anxiety disorders do not have a biological defect. They have a spirit of Fear, which they either inherited or it came into them through their life circumstances.

FEAR OF PARENTS AND YOUR KIDS

Do you know how many people are afraid of their parents or their kids? How about Fear of Rejection by a child? Do you know how many parents are in child idolatry where the child rules the home? Most parents who go into child idolatry failed in their own lives, so the child becomes an extension of their damaged egos.

When the child is successful, the parents feel they too are a success. The child must be the "success" of their failure. Do you know how accurate this assessment is? Behind every person's action there is a motivating thought. Did it come from God, or did it come from the devil, or is it just misguided ignorance?

Are your thoughts:
from God
from the devil
or from yourself

Do you know how many boys are "Mama's boys?" Do you know how many women come to me and say their husband's mother is more important to him than she is, as his wife?

When Mama calls he jumps, but when wifey calls he watches football all day. He has to live near Mama because he was a surrogate husband, since his daddy was never emotionally or spiritually there.

The mother had such a need that the son became a surrogate emotional (not sexual) husband. It stayed that way for the rest of their days, and he is now the spiritual head of his Mama, instead of being the spiritual head of his wife. In this case, the boy is following his Mama.

But most of the time, the husband follows the wife, who has to live near her Mama. Families usually congregate around where the wife's mother lives, not where the husband wants to be and not where God has sent him. Where you find Mama you will find the family. If Mama is controlling the family at this level, that is matriarchal control.

The Bible says when you get married, you are to leave mother and father and cleave one to another. There can be an ungodly spiritual reality where the man is not following God, because he is bound to where his wife wants to be. Now there is nothing wrong with considering each other's wishes, but we are dealing with Fear here.

You might look in your *Strong's Concordance* on *fear, fearfulness, afraid,* and do your own word study sometime. The Word of God will speak to you. Nowhere in the Bible does it tell you to be afraid, but it will give you many examples of people who were.

FEAR OF PAIN

Fear of Pain can produce pain.

FEAR OF POVERTY

Many people have a spirit of Poverty and Fear of Poverty. When they are given something they feel guilty. I know the Bible says it is better to give than to receive, but it is also just as important to receive. Did you receive God's love? Do you feel guilty about it?

If I come up and say, "I love you," do you feel guilty? If you do, that would be an unclean, Unloving spirit. If I gave you a million dollars today, would you feel guilty about it? You might. You might be afraid of what other people would think of you. That would be Fear of man.

Or you might be greedy, but Greed comes under Envy and Jealousy. Greed also can be motivated by Fear of poverty, which will produce a miserly spirit. That "Scrooge" spirit comes out of Fear of Poverty.

Food, raiment and housing are basic requirements of life: food for sustenance, clothing for bodily protection from heat and cold and a house to protect you from enemies and the elements. These are all necessities.

We all need a place to sleep, a place to live, a place to hang out, or just do whatever. That is what life is really all about. Most of the time, your fears are around not having what you need in these three areas.

Another Fear that produces compulsive spending, shoplifting and kleptomania is rooted in an Unloving spirit and comes out of the Fear of not having enough.

FEAR OF REPROACH FROM MEN

There is Fear of the reproach of men. The following scenario demonstrates Reproach.

"Well, I think we ought to paint the walls green."

"Well, you dumb old thing. Are you color blind or what? They should be painted pink."

What just happened to you? You have been reproached. You have been rejected. What if you are going on a drive with someone and you say, "Well, I think this is the shortest way to get there."

"Well, what's the matter with you, man? I have driven this road many times. This is the way." You have just been reproached.

Have you ever gone to your spouse or to your parents with a wonderful, fantastic idea that you are very excited about and they trashed it instantly? Is that reproach? Do you have a Fear of approaching them again? Yes, because you have Fear of reproach.

Isaiah says,

> **Hearken unto me, ye that know righteousness, the people in whose heart *is* my law; fear ye not the reproach of men, neither be ye afraid of their revilings.** Isaiah 51:7

Webster's Dictionary defines "reproach:" to accuse of and blame for a fault so as to make one feel ashamed; to rebuke or to reprove; to bring shame upon; disgrace; discredit; to bring reproof or blame.

Have you ever been blamed for something? That is a form of reproach. The word "reproach" is also used in the context of Jesus being rejected of men. How many times do you not approach people because of Fear of reproach or Fear of being shamed?

FEAR OF REPROOF

The Bible says, "An open rebuke is better than secret love." Proverbs 27:5 Reproof is when someone says you have done something that is not exactly the way it should be done. You are told you need to do it differently. You have been reproved.

"What shall I say when God reproves me?" Habakkuk 2:1 tells you what to do. You make a new plan, get on with it, and do it right. It is as simple as that.

> **I will stand upon my watch, and set me upon the tower, and will watch to see what he will say unto me, and what I shall answer when I am reproved.** Habakkuk 2:1

FEAR OF RESPONSIBILITY

I was reading about Miss Wolfe, Carl Jung's mistress of forty years, and his progression into polygamy. Carl Jung taught polygamy as a liberating way of life. He learned this from another psychotherapist. He had a mistress who became his close associate and she became unable to care for herself.

Even after he died, she had either a sister, or a mother, or a maid. She cooked no meals. She did no housecleaning. She wanted to be taken care of and she had no responsibilities. Would you say she had a Fear of responsibility? She always found someone who would cater to her and take care of her, because she refused to take care of herself.

FEAR OF SEX

Fear of your sexuality is not the same thing as having Fear of sex. How about Fear of having sex or the loss of it? There could be Fear of loneliness or Fear of pregnancy.

Fear of sex also includes Fear of intercourse, but Fear of intercourse may be because there is pain involved. It could come out of victimization or a biological problem. Sometimes sex is painful because of lack of lubrication due to frigidity, anxiety or loss of libido.

There is a whole mixture of things that come out of proper relationship here. This is not an unclean subject. This is life and it needs to be discussed openly, because what you do not discuss openly becomes a phobia.

What you do not bring out in the light becomes a phobia

FEAR OF SEXUALITY

Many people deal with Fear of their own sexuality. Many people cannot have sex with the lights on because they are so ashamed of their bodies. That is rooted in Self-Hatred and Shame, as well as Fear.

When Adam and Eve were created, they were naked. When they sinned, Shame came and they went and hid and said, "We are naked."

God said to them, "Who told you you were naked? You are not supposed to know that."

In that moment, we see in creation the human body is not evil and the human body is not unclean. The human body was created perfect from the beginning. Now what made it unclean? Perverse spirits.

Maybe your parents put the Shame into you. Many mommies and daddies have scarred their children, made them full of Shame and taught them that sexuality was dirty.

You should teach your children there is a timing of life and relationship when sex occurs in marriage. You prepare them for the fulfillment, but you do not teach it from the standpoint of it being unclean. Teach sex from the standpoint of godly order in procreation and in relationship.

Pornography is a very abusive industry. It demeans the female, making her an object of the flesh. A woman's sexuality is not as an object of the flesh. A woman's sexuality is who she is.

There is nothing wrong with a woman's sexuality. It is very beautiful. There is nothing wrong with a man's sexuality, providing it is within the boundaries of what God has created it to be, without perverseness or inordinate affection.

What about Fear of someone else's sexuality? Fear of your own sexuality is rooted in feeling unclean, in not feeling like you are a whole person. Fear of another's sexuality is the fruit of molestation. Then you have the Fear of Victimization, which is also the Fear of another's sexuality.

The marriage bed is undefiled, provided you do not take anything from one another. You only receive what is given to you. Anything that is taken is evil, but anything that is given is a gift.

The Bible says the power of the man's body does not belong to him; it belongs to his wife. The power of the wife's body does not belong to her; her body belongs to her husband. 1 Corinthians 7:4 They cannot *take* from one another; they only *receive* what is given to them.

Sometimes Lust takes over and man becomes evil and barbaric. Lust never fulfills anything; it only takes for self-fulfillment. You should only receive what is freely given to you. Fear of another's sexuality and Fear of your own sexuality manifests as frigidity or impotence.

FEAR OF SMELLS

Fear of smells would be allergic reactions.

FEAR OF SPOUSE

Fear of your husband, Fear of your wife. A lot of men are afraid of their wives and a lot of wives are afraid of their husbands.

FEAR OF UNKNOWN

Fear of the unknown is a sin. Matthew 6:34 says, "Take no thought for tomorrow."

FEAR OF VERBAL REJECTION

"Neither be ye afraid of their revilings," which are verbal rejections. Have you ever avoided your pastor because you were afraid of verbal rejection? Come on now, this is "pastor-phobia" time. That is Fear of authority or Fear of pastors.

FEAR OF WAR

Many people are afraid of war, but the book of Psalms says,

> **Though an host should encamp against me, my heart shall not fear: though war should rise against me, in this *will* I *be* confident.** Psalm 27:3

Let God be God and keep your peace. Make no attempt to defend yourself when there are wars in your life. War is a battle with what is in someone else.

Have you ever had anyone gang up on you and turn against you? Sure. Maintain your confidence, because God is your source.

HORROR

The book of Psalms says,

> **My heart is sore pained within me: and the terrors of death are fallen upon me. Fearfulness and trembling are come upon me, and horror hath overwhelmed me.** Psalm 55:4-5

Do you know how many times in ministry I have had to deal with a spirit of Horror? Horror is a type of Fear. Where do you get the spirit of Horror? Horror movies bring fearfulness; trembling would be a physiological fruit.

HORROR MOVIES

Once I ministered to a child who was having nightmares after watching *Murder on Elm Street*, with Freddy Krueger. I said, "You have an evil spirit. In fact, I can get it to manifest just by calling it 'Freddy.' " Even though its name is not Freddy, the spirit of Fear and Torment that was behind that movie was transferred to the child.

"I am going to command the evil spirit to come up in you," I said, "and I am going to just call it Freddy, because that was the medium."

"You evil spirit that came into this child through the character of Freddy, I command you to manifest and to come out in the name of Jesus." And the child went white and stood there and trembled and shook. It was as if he had palsy and was having a fit and couldn't stop. Then the spirit came out.

If you watched movies like that as a child, you have some problems. If you allow your children to watch them, they will have problems. You need to allow God to bring to your remembrance everything you have allowed yourself to be exposed to, from childhood on, that would have been an open door for Fear.

That includes every horror flick you have ever watched. You are going to have to repent to God for allowing it access to your soul, because that is exactly what the devil uses.

HYPOCRITICAL LOVE

Have you ever put on a hypocritical love act because you did not want to show that you did not really care that much? False love is a tremendous Fear item. It is a form of hypocrisy. You do not want to offend someone; you do not want to tell your real feelings. In your heart you're thinking, "I just really hate your guts." So what do you do? You come out with this false piety, this false reality. You act like it is okay. That is Fear of man.

INFERIORITY

Inferiority is a type of Fear.

NIGHT TORMENT

What was happening to Job when he said, "In thoughts from the visions of the night, when deep sleep falleth on men..."? Job was asleep and he was having a dream, a vision. What kind of dream was it? "Fear came upon me." He was having a nightmare! "Fear came upon me and trembling which made all my bones to shake, and then a spirit passed before my face." Job 4:13-15 An evil spirit was involved with that nightmare.

Tormenting nightmares that put Fear into you are the work of an evil spirit. It is not just coming out of your consciousness, but out of your spirit. It comes from beyond the realm of consciousness and is a tormenting spirit that has come into you and is part of your life.

The only way you can be free of night torment is to be delivered. Now the doorpoint is very important. Many children watch horror movies and they are filled with evil spirits of Fear. You need to be very careful what you watch. Spirits use these mediums of expression to contact people, and there can be transference of spirits.

PHOBIAS

There are a lot of phobias. I will list a few of them: Fear of airplanes, ambulances, animals, babies, Fear of being alone, Fear of being discovered, Fear of bridges, Fear of cancer (that would be Fear of disease), Fear of cats, Fear of childbirth, Fear of choking, Fear of confinement, Fear of crowds, Fear of death, Fear of deliverance, Fear of evil spirits, Fear of evil, Fear of dogs, Fear of driving, Fear of elevators, Fear of embarrassment, Fear of Failure, Fear of falling, Fear of the future, Fear of germs, Fear of getting hurt, Fear of giving love, Fear of receiving love, Fear of heart attacks, Fear of heights, Fear of hurting people.

SELF-AWARENESS

Self-Awareness comes out of Fear.

SHYNESS

Shyness is withdrawing; it is an action of Fear.

SPECULATIVE FEARS

Have you ever had a thought, then immediately projected the Fear concerning it, but there wasn't anything happening in your life around that issue? Fear of nothing would be just general anxiety, but speculative Fear has an object. For example, if I am walking and something is in my path, speculative Fear says, "You are going to trip over this thing, fall and break your neck."

There are two kinds of speculative fears: one where you are anticipating or speculating that something might happen tomorrow; and precognition—or clairvoyance—related to an event not yet experienced. This occurs when a spirit of Fear is trying to fulfill itself.

I dealt with a pastor who played with an Ouija board at age 18 that told him he would die at age 34. Guess what has been tormenting him all these years? He became so phobic he increased his life insurance for his wife and family to make provision for his death. Someone in his church was healed through this ministry; then a second person in his church was healed through this ministry.

The next thing you know, I am talking to both him and his wife on the phone. Over a period of time they came to recognize that an evil spirit of Death was trying to be fulfilled through his Fear and we had to cancel it. The devil is a liar. God is true.

The Bible says if people prophesy the future and it does not come to pass, you are not to be afraid of them or listen to them in anything. Anyone from God, in the area of a prophetic statement in the name of the Lord, cannot be wrong one time. If they are wrong one time, they have Divination.

The Bible was written by holy men and prophets, and every word they spoke was right from the throne of God by the Holy Spirit. 2 Peter 1:21 Jesus confirmed that, and His disciples confirmed that. The Word says a prophet or prophetess cannot be wrong in foretelling *one time.* If they are, you do not have to fear them; they are not of God. They are either prophesying out of their own spirit or they are prophesying out of the spirit of the devil.

Can prophets or men of God come and God speak to us through them? There is much evidence it is true. But in the Christian church today, especially in the churches that are filled with Divination, everyone is giving each other prophecies and personal words of knowledge. About 90 percent of it is of the devil. How can you know? You have to try the spirits: whether or not they are of God. 1 John 4:1

SUPERSTITIONS

How about superstitions? What about, "Step on a crack, break your mother's back?" When I am walking down the sidewalk, I step on every crack I can. I say, "Take that, devil. I cast down that superstition."

When I see a ladder against the side of the building, I look first to make sure the guy on it does not have a bucket of paint. I walk under it and say, "Take that devil, so much for superstition." When a mirror breaks, what do I do? Throw it in the garbage.

UNBELIEF AND DOUBT

Unbelief and Doubt is an antichrist spirit, too. God's Word tells us not to fear because He highly values us and will not forget us.

> **...for he hath said, I will never leave thee, nor forsake thee.**
> Hebrews 13:5

FEAR LIST

Fear of aging. Fear of menopause. Fear of drowning. Fear of suffocation. Fear of fires. Fear of lightning. Fear of electrocution. Fear of storms. Fear of heights. Fear of elevators. Fear of crowds. Fear of being free. Fear of God.

Fear of airplanes, ambulances, animals, babies. Fear of bridges. Fear of being alone. Fear of childbirth. Fear of choking. Fear of confinement.

Fear of dependency. Fear of betrayal. Fear of being trapped in circumstances. Fear of criticism. Fear of disapproval.

Fear of doctors and hospitals. Fear of white coats. Fear of bad news. Fear of needles. Fear of change. Fear of vomiting. Fear of disability.

Introspection. Self-Consciousness. Self-Awareness. Oversensitivity. Timidity. Apprehension.

Fear of inadequacy. Fear of intimacy. Fear of public speaking—which is Fear of man. Feelings of distress—which would be an unknown Fear.

Fear of insects. Fear of intimacy. Fear of noises.

Fear of judgment against yourself, God, or anyone else. Fear of loss of identity. Fear of making a commitment. Fear of marriage. Fear of men. Fear of situations.

Fear of nuclear war. Fear of Pain. Fear of radiation. Fear of rape. Fear of suffocation. Fear of water. Fear of women.

Fear of Accusation. Fear of condemnation. Fear of harassment. Fear of persecutions and suffering. Fear of disfigurement. Fear of blood. Fear of not having your turn at the washer and dryer.

Fear of thieves. Fear of being robbed. Fear of staying home. Fear of weapons.

You may have to deal with many of these Fears. Do you wonder why you are having bad nights, and insomnia has a chance at you?

No wonder!

The hypothalamus gland is the seat for all Fear, anxiety, stress, panic, phobias, Rage and Anger. It is one of the centers for sleep, thirst and eating. So one master gland controls a wide range of actions that can all be affected by how you think. That is the mind-body connection.

In your heart, you know your enemy, don't you?

Come before the Lord with your personal list, hold it up to God and let the devil know you are not going to put up with this stuff anymore. Let him know you are going to take your life back.

We are stripping away his armor. "The strong man armed keepeth his palace; his goods are in peace, but when one stronger than he comes upon him, he strips from him all the armor in which he trusts." Luke 11:21 The principality of Fear is banking on the fact that he can control you through this type of armor.

It has to be stripped away so that the strong man of Fear can be defeated in your life. Would you like to have a heart full of faith and not Fear? Then take authority over Fear and set some things into motion in the spirit.

Set in motion that God is working with you and you are working with God, so your enemy cannot control you. Day by day you will walk away from many of these areas of your life and that will be to God's glory and for your benefit. Amen? Amen!

Practical Steps to Freedom

If you want to be free of Fear, let me suggest the following steps as a very effective place to start. This is how you can walk out and be free.

1. Make a Decision

Make a decision. Speak it out to God that you do not accept Fear in your life anymore and you want your life to be in agreement with His Word. You have to come to the place where you make that bold declaration. That has to happen first. You have to make that decision to turn away from Fear.

2. Ask for Discernment

Ask God for discernment so that you may see more clearly how you are being affected by Fear. If you do not understand Fear, make sure you look at it more closely. If you identify with it, Fear is part of your life. It has to go. Tell God, "I am not going to have Fear of Abandonment." Tell your Father in heaven, "I need your help." Then tell your enemy, "You are not going to live my life any more."

3. Repent

Repent to God specifically for each way you have given in to Fear, not trusted Him and not believed His Word. You have to do that when Fear is present. You may think you can be delivered from Fear and *then* repent to God. No, you repent to God *first*.

4. Ask God to Forgive You

Ask God to forgive you when you sin. Ask God to work in your heart, so you may begin to truly trust and believe Him and be free from Fear. Ask God to forgive you.

5. Develop New Habits

Walk in this every day. You are breaking old habits by developing new ones. That is what science says about the programming of your mind. You can establish new memes that will replace the old ones and the new memes will become the standard for your life.

When the spirit of Fear comes around again, you are filled with the knowledge of God and you are walking in it. Walk in it every day and repent whenever you recognize you are in Fear, and ask God to deliver you from this Fear.

6. Quote the Word

When Fear tries to come, quote the Word to him. Quote it to yourself. Tell your mind, "Listen to me. Wake up."

Paul said to Timothy,

> **For God hath not given us the spirit of fear; but of power, and of love, and of a sound mind.** 2 Timothy 1:7

Declare over your life that you believe these words from God and will not believe what Fear is saying to you any more.

7. CHOOSE WHAT YOU WILL BELIEVE

Every time you recognize Fear rising up you have to respond with what you are going to believe. When you believe God's Word and declare it—when you trust God and believe Him—He will protect and care for you and save you out of all of your troubles.

Or you may choose to believe Fear, which speaks against the Word of God. You have to continually choose to believe God no matter what things may look like to your natural eyes, or seem like to your natural mind. This is what is required to defeat Fear in your life. Then you will have a living faith and will see the Word of God come to pass in your life.

> **The LORD *is* my light and my salvation; whom shall I fear? the LORD *is* the strength of my life; of whom shall I be afraid?** Psalm 27:1

Renouncing Fear

You may need to talk to yourself (and the creature) and say:

> Fear, you are a creature. You are going to get out of here. I am going to take a look at you in my life because the Word of God says there is no creature that is not made manifest before Him with whom I have to do.
>
> The Word of God is quick and powerful, sharper than a two-edged sword, is a discerner of the thoughts, and intents and the feelings of my heart and I want you exposed. The Word is going to show me that you are a liar. Now get out of here. You are not going to control me any longer. God said He did not give me a spirit of Fear, so you have no right to be here.

The antidote to Fear is the Godhead: the Father; the Word, who is Jesus Christ of Nazareth; and the Holy Spirit. Stand up and say,

> My Father is in heaven on the throne. Jesus Christ is God the Word and He came in the flesh and died for my sins. He spoiled principalities and powers and made a show of them openly. He took the keys to death, hell and the grave. He is my Redeemer and my Savior and my Deliverer; I have Him and His Word in my heart.
>
> I am sealed by the Holy Spirit which reveals the will of God the Father to me as the Word of God. He is able to keep those things that I have committed. He is my Comforter and He is the One that leads me into all truth. He is the Power of God. You have to flee! Now, go!

Related Reading

If you have found this book helpful, we suggest the following additional teachings. All are available from the website www.beinhealth.com.

A More Excellent Way™, Henry Wright's foundational book on the spiritual roots of disease and blocks to healing

Seven Steps to Sin

8Rs to Freedom

Walking Out to Wholeness

Bitterness

Envy and Jealousy

Rejection

Unloving

Fear, Stress and Physiology

Insights into Allergies